# WARRIOR WISDOM
## Inspiring Ideas from the World's Greatest Warriors

By
**Sammy Franco**

**CONTEMPORARY FIGHTING ARTS, LLC.**

**Also by Sammy Franco:**
Judge, Jury and Executioner
Savage Street Fighting: Tactical Savagery as a Last Resort
Feral Fighting: Level 2 WidowMaker
Ground War: How to Destroy a Grappler in a Street Fight
The Combat Conditioning Workout Journal
War Blade: A Complete Guide to Tactical Knife Fighting
The WidowMaker Program: Maximum Punishment for Extreme Situations
War Craft: Street Fighting Tactics of the War Machine
War Machine: Transform Yourself into a Vicious & Deadly Street Fighter
The Bigger They Are, The Harder They Fall
First Strike: Mastering the Pre-Emptive Strike for Street Combat
1001 Street Fighting Secrets: The Principles of Contemporary Fighting Arts
When Seconds Count: Everyone's Guide to Self-Defense
Killer Instinct: Unarmed Combat for Street Survival
Street Lethal: Unarmed Urban Combat

**Warrior Wisdom by Sammy Franco**
Copyright © 2011 by Sammy Franco
ISBN 0-9818721-9-0
Printed in the United States of America


Published by Contemporary Fighting Arts, LLC.
P.O. Box 84028
Gaithersburg, Maryland 20883 USA
Call Toll Free: 1-(877) 232-3334
Visit us online at: www.sammyfranco.com

# Table of Contents

INTRODUCTION      1

CHAPTER 1: COURAGE & FEAR      2

CHAPTER 2: LEADERSHIP      21

CHAPTER 3: LOYALTY      45

CHAPTER 4: TACTICS AND STRATEGY      53

CHAPTER 5: HONOR      99

CHAPTER 6: SELF-CONTROL & PERSEVERANCE      112

CHAPTER 7: WISDOM, FAITH AND BELIEF      130

CHAPTER 8: MISCELLANEOUS BUT MEMORABLE      152

CHAPTER 9: QUOTES FROM THE AUTHOR      183

BIOGRAPHIES      193

ABOUT THE AUTHOR      210

# Introduction

As long as humankind has recorded the written word, the warrior has been admired as the embodiment of some of the best aspects of human beings. They have demanded and demonstrated the great qualities and possibilities of moral human action such as courage, loyalty, determination and intelligence. Writers of all kinds and natures have recorded the deeds of these great warriors as models of valiant behavior and chivalrous ideals.

These great warriors lived on the knife edge between life and death, and their pending mortality acted to reveal eternal truths about human life through both their motives and acts. Thus the warrior perspective is universally unique and therefore still applicable today in our more complex modern world.

Here then is a collection of writings from warriors and warrior leaders, both past and present, and from around the world. They reveal the essentialities of the Fighter's life, speaking with great heart, eloquence, wisdom and an earned authenticity on subjects still crucial to you today: leadership, loyalty, honour, courage and much more. Read what warriors – Western and Eastern, obscure and famous, admirable and despicable – have said about themselves and others. Be inspired by the words of such important figures from Alexander the Great to General Patton. Benefit from the pithy strategic wisdoms of Xenophon, Miyamoto Musahi, Sun Tzu and Napoleon Bonaparte. Enjoy the wit of Winston Churchill and the philosophical and spiritual musings of Marcus Aurelius and King David.

# Chapter 1
# Courage and Fear

*C*ourage is at the essential core of any hero. Courage both inspires and validates the warrior. In all times and in all places, courage has been admired and revered, and has become the reason and the rationale for a society's success. But precisely what is courage? In many ways, it is easier to say what courage is not. Courage is not recklessness or foolish risk-taking, nor is it haphazard rage and fury. Instead, courage breeds confidence, resolution and bravery. As many a fighter will tell you, fear can be intimately entwined with courage. Fear is the stimulus that, biologically speaking, triggers the fight-or-flight response; yet courage is choosing to stay and fight rather than to run away.

---

"The bravest are surely those who have the clearest vision of what is before them, glory and danger alike, and yet notwithstanding, go out to meet it." -**Thucydides**

"The principle on which to manage an army is to set up one standard of courage which all must reach." -**Sun Tzu**

"The fate of unborn millions will now depend, under God, on the courage and conduct of this army. Our cruel and unrelenting enemy leaves us only the choice of brave resistance, or the most abject submission. We have, therefore, to resolve to conquer or die." -**George Washington**

"One man with courage makes a majority." -**Andrew Jackson**

"Courage is what it takes to stand up and speak; courage is also what it takes to sit down and listen." **-Winston Churchill**

"Courage brother, do not stumble, though thy path be dark as night: There is a star to guide the humble, trust in God, and do the right. Let the road be dark and dreary and its end far out of sight. Face it bravely, strong or weary. Trust God..."
**-General Norman Schwarzkopf**

"We have nothing left in the world but what we can win with our swords. Timidity and cowardice are for men who can see safety at their backs - who can retreat without molestation along some easy road and find refuge in the familiar fields of their native land; but they are not for you: you must be brave; for you there is no middle way between victory or death - put all hope of it from you, and either conquer, or, should fortune hesitate to favour you, meet death in battle rather than in flight." **-Hannibal**

"I dislike death; however, there are some things I dislike more than death. Therefore, there are times when I will not avoid danger." **-Mencius**

"The battle of Iwo Island [Jima] has been won. The United States Marines, by their individual and collective courage, have conquered a base which is as necessary to us in our continuing forward movement toward final victory as it was vital to the enemy in staving off ultimate defeat.... Among the Americans who served on Iwo Island, uncommon valor was a common virtue." **-Fleet Admiral Chester W. Nimitz**

"No guts; no glory." **-Major Frederick Blesse**

"No matter whether a person belongs to the upper or lower ranks, if he has not put his life on the line at least once he has cause for shame." **-Nabeshima Naoshige**

"One finds life through conquering the fear of death within one's mind. Empty the mind of all forms of attachment, make a go-for-broke charge and conquer the opponent with one decisive slash." -**Togo Shigekata**

"If you're afraid of anything, why not take a chance and do the thing you fear? Sometimes it's the only way to get over being afraid." -**Audie Murphy**

"A true knight is fuller of bravery in the midst, than in the beginning of danger."
-**Philip Sidney**

"In battle it is the cowards who run the most risk; bravery is a rampart of defense."
-**Sallust**

"Seems to me that if you're afraid or living with some big fear, you're not really living. You're only half alive. I don't care if it's the boss you're scared of or a lot of people in a room or diving off of a dinky little board, you gotta get rid of it. You owe it to yourself. Makes sort of a zombie out of you, being afraid. I mean you want to be free, don't you? And how can you if you are scared? That's prison. Fear's a jailer. Mind now, I'm not a professor on the subject. I just found it out for myself. But that's what I think."
-**Audie Murphy**

"Taking advantage of their fright and fear is the means by which one can attack ten."
-**Jiang Taigong**

"Courage is rightly esteemed the first of human qualities, because… it is the quality that guarantees all others." -**Winston Churchill**

"Let bravery be thy choice, but not bravado." -**Menander**

"The way I see it, if you're scared of something you'd better get busy and do something about it. I'd call that a challenge – and I believe that the way to grow is to meet all the challenges as they come along." -**Audie Murphy**

"Nature has set nothing so high that it cannot be surmounted by courage. It is by using methods of which others have despaired that we have Asia in our power."
-**Alexander the Great**

"With our army all fervently engaging in battle, the enemy shall certainly be defeated."
-**Jiang Taigong**

"It is not numbers, but bravery which carries the day."
-**Publius Flavius Vegetius Renatus**

"The courageous love to put their ambition into effect." -**Huang Shi Gong**

"Within the army, there will be soldiers whose courage is that of the tiger, has strength that can lift tripods easily and has the fleetness of a barbarian horse. To seize enemy's flag or kill the enemy's generals, you need such men. You should select them and put them into one unit, honor and favour them. This is because in their hands hold the fate of the whole army." -**Wu Qi**

"I'll tell you what bravery really is. Bravery is just the determination to do a job that you know has to be done." -**Audie Murphy**

"And above all you ought to guard against leading an army to fight which is afraid or which is not confident of victory. For the greatest sign of an impending loss is when one does not believe one can win." -**Machiavelli**

"For as the well trained soldier is eager for action, so does the untaught fear it."
-**Publius Flavius Vegetius Renatus**

"Fear makes men forget, and skill which cannot fight is useless." -**Brasides of Sparta**

"Within the army, there will be men with great courage and strength who are willing to die and may even take pleasure in suffering wounds. They should be assembled together and called 'Warriors who Risks the Blade'. Those who have very fierce disposition, who are robust and courageous, strong and explosive, should be assembled together and called 'Warriors who Penetrate the Lines'. Those who are extraordinary in appearance, bear long swords and advance with measured tread in good order should be assembled together and called 'Courageous Elite Warriors'. Those who can straighten iron hooks, have great strength, and can go into enemy's line and smash gongs and drums and destroy flags and pennants, should be assembled together and called 'Warriors of Courage and Strength." -**Jiang Taigong**

"Your equipment is the key, while courageous fighting is foremost." -**Jiang Taigong**

"It seems to be a law of nature, inflexible and inexorable, that those who will not risk cannot win." -**Admiral John Paul Jones**

"Whoever wants to see his own people again must remember to be a brave soldier: that is the only way of doing it. Whoever wants to keep alive must aim at victory. It is the winners who do the killing and the losers who get killed." -**Xenophon**

"Like timidity, bravery is also contagious." -**Munshi Premchand**

"I have not yet begun to fight!" -**Admiral John Paul Jones**

"If you fight to be strong, the strong can be conquered. If you can attain complete victory without fighting, without the great army suffering any losses, you will have penetrated even the realm of ghosts and spirits. How marvellous! How subtle!"
**-Jiang Taigong**

"What counts is not necessarily the size of the dog in the fight – it's the size of the fight in the dog." **-Dwight D. Eisenhower**

"History does not long entrust the care of freedom to the weak or the timid."
**-Dwight D. Eisenhower**

"True courage is being afraid, and going ahead and doing your job."
**- General Norman Schwarzkopf**

"Commitment means entering combat without any concern for one's life." **-Wu Qi**

"Bravery is the capacity to perform properly even when scared half to death."
**-Omar Bradley**

"A brave captain is a root, out which as branches the courage of his soldiers."
**-Sir Philip Sidney**

"To dilute the will to win is to destroy the purpose of the game. There is no substitute for victory." **-Douglas MacArthur**

"They are in front of us, behind us, and we are flanked on both sides by an enemy that outnumbers us twenty-nine to one. They can't get away from us now!"
**-Lewis Burwell "Chesty" Puller**

"It is natural for men in general to be affected with some sensations of fear at the beginning of an engagement, but there are without doubt some of a more timorous disposition who are disordered by the very sight of the enemy. To diminish these apprehensions before you venture on action, draw up your army frequently in order of battle in some safe situation, so that your men may be accustomed to the sight and appearance of the enemy. When opportunity offers, they should be sent to fall upon them and endeavor to put them to flight or kill some of their men. Thus they will become acquainted with their customs, arms and horses. And the objects with which we are once familiarized are no longer capable of inspiring us with terror."
**-Publius Flavius Vegetius Renatus**


"Fear is a reaction. Courage is a decision." **-Winston Churchill**


"Though an army should encamp against me, my heart shall not fear; though war should rise against me, in this I will be confident." **-King David**


"Last, but by no means least, courage – moral courage, the courage of one's convictions, the courage to see things through the world – is in a constant conspiracy against the brave. It's the age-old struggle: the roar of the crowd on one side and the voice of your conscience on the other." **-Douglas MacArthur**


"Goddam it, you'll never get the Purple Heart hiding in a foxhole! Follow me!"
**-Captain Henry P. "Jim" Crowe, USMC, Guadalcanal, 13 January 1943.**


"You are well aware that it is not numbers or strength that bring the victories in war. No, it is when one side goes against the enemy with the gods' gift of a stronger morale that their adversaries, as a rule cannot withstand them. I have noticed this point, too, my friends, that in soldiering, the people whose one aim is to keep alive usually find a wretched and dishonorable death, while the people who, realizing that death is the common lot of all men, make it their endeavor to die with honor, somehow seem more often to reach old age and to have a happier life while they are alive." **-Xenophon**

"Generals unskilled in war think a victory incomplete unless the enemy are so straightened in their ground or so entirely surrounded by numbers as to have no possibility of escape. But in such situation, where no hopes remain, fear itself will arm an enemy and despair inspires courage. When men find they must inevitably perish, they willingly resolve to die with their comrades and with their arms in their hands."
**-Publius Flavius Vegetius Renatus**

"Go to the battlefield firmly confident of victory and you will come home with no wounds whatsoever." **-Uesugi Kenshin**

"The cowards never start and the weak die along the way."
**-Christopher Houston "Kit" Carson**

"The exceptional man may not feel fear, but the great mass of men do - their nervous control alone stands between them and a complete yielding to fear.

This nervous control may be upset in two principal ways. It may be worn thin by a long-continued strain - it may be shattered in a single instant by sudden shock. Usually it gives under a combin-ation of these influences. The control is worn away imperceptibly by the anxiety and suspense of waiting for the enemy's blow, by the noise and concussive effect of shellfire, and by loss of the sleep that renovates the tired will. Then without warning the shock of a sudden surprise danger snaps the fine drawn thread of the will to resist. Stubborn resistance changes in a moment to panic-stricken flight. Fear becomes uncontrollable terror." **-Captain Sir Basil Liddell Hart**

"There are risks and costs to a program of action, but they are far less than the long-range risks and costs of comfortable inaction." **-John F Kennedy**

"For it is the soldier's disposition to offer an obstinate resistance when surrounded, to fight hard when he cannot help himself, and to obey promptly when he has fallen into danger." -**Sun Tzu**

"If there is a villain who is sentenced to death but has escaped and he is hiding. One thousand men have been sent to look for him and they just look around for him. Why? This is because they are afraid that the villain would inflict personal harm to them. Thus a man who disregards death can frighten a thousand. Now if I can take a mass of fifty thousand and gather them into a single murderous villain... we will surely make it difficult for the enemy." -**Wu Qi**

"You must not fear death, my lads; defy him, and you drive him into the enemy's ranks."-**Napoleon Bonaparte**

"With audacity one can undertake anything, but not do everything."
-**Napoleon Bonaparte**

"Courage is like love; it must have hope for nourishment."
-**Napoleon Bonaparte**

"He who fears being conquered is sure of defeat."
-**Napoleon Bonaparte**

"The Romans also have an excellent method of encouraging young soldiers to face danger. Whenever any have especially distinguished themselves in a battle, the general assembles the troops and calls forward those he considers to have shown exceptional courage. He praises them first for their gallantry in action and for anything in their previous conduct which is particularly worthy of mention, and then he distributes gifts... These presentations are not made to men who have wounded or stripped an enemy in the course of a pitched battle, or at the storming of a city, but to those who during a skirmish or some similar situation in which there is no necessity to engage in single combat, have voluntarily and deliberately exposed themselves to danger." -**Polybius**

"Untutored courage is useless in the face of educated bullets." -**General Patton**

"All men are timid on entering any fight. Whether it is the first or the last fight, all of us are timid. Cowards are those who let their timidity get the better of their manhood."
-**General Patton**

"Courage is fear holding on a minute longer." -**General Patton**

"There is a time to take counsel of your fears, and there is a time to never listen to any fear." -**General Patton**

"You are not all going to die. Only two percent of you here, in a major battle would die. Death must not be feared. Every man is frightened at first in battle. If he says he isn't he is a God damn liar. Some men are cowards, yes, but they fight just the same or get the hell scared out of them watching men who do fight and who are just as scared as they. The real hero is the man who fights even though he is scared. Some get over their fright in a few minutes under fire, some take hours, some take days. The real man never lets the fear of death over-power his honor, his duty to his country and his innate manhood."
-**General Patton, speech to the Third Army.**

"Accept the challenges so that you can feel the exhilaration of victory."
-**General Patton**

"It often requires more courage to dare to do right than to fear to do wrong."
-**Abraham Lincoln**

"It is courage, courage, courage, that raises the blood of life to crimson splendor. Live bravely and present a brave front to adversity." -**Horace**

"Generally speaking, the Way of the warrior is resolute acceptance of death."
-**Miyamoto Musashi**

"The battle, sir, is not to the strong alone; it is to the vigilant, the active, the brave."
-**Patrick Henry**

"The secret of happiness is freedom. The secret of freedom is courage." -**Thucydides**

"The strong do what they have to do and the weak accept what they have to accept."
-**Thucydides**

"Be convinced that to be happy means to be free and that to be free means to be brave. Therefore do not take lightly the perils of war." -**Thucydides**

"For not by numbers of men, nor by measure of body, but by valor of soul is war to be decided." -**Belisarius**

"Cowards die many times before their actual deaths." -**Julius Caesar**

"It is bad policy to fear the resentment of an enemy." -**Ethan Allen**

"A man of character in peace is a man of courage in war." -**Lord Moran**

"Courage is a moral quality; it is not a chance gift of nature like an aptitude for games. It is a cold choice between two alternatives, the fixed resolve not to quit; an act of renunciation which must be made not once but many times by the power of the will. Courage is willpower." -**Lord Moran**


"Fear is apparently a formidable alley for a guard." -**Xenophon**


"Let me assert my firm belief that the only thing we have to fear is fear itself."
-**Franklin D. Roosevelt**


"Very few men are born brave, but any man can make himself brave if he tries."
-**Robert Baden-Powell**


"The desire for safety stands against every great and noble enterprise." -**Tacitus**


"It is not death that a man should fear, but he should fear never beginning to live."
-**Marcus Aurelius**


"No man is worth his salt who is not ready at all times to risk his body, to risk his well-being, to risk his life in a great cause." -**Theodore Roosevelt**


"The Germans will doubtless attack again.  Let every man work and stay alert to achieve the same success as yesterday… Courage!  We will take them!"
-**General Philippe Petain**


"It's only a mortar!  Get the bastard." -**Lt Col. Tiwi Love**

"Fellow citizens, I am being besieged by a thousand or more Mexicans... the enemy have demanded a surrender at discretion, otherwise the garrison is to be put to the sword, if the fort is taken. I have answered the demand with a cannon shot, and our flag still waves proudly from the walls. I shall never surrender nor retreat... Victory or Death!"
**-Lt. Col. W. Barrett Travis**


"If an enemy were firing down this street, and you had to take a message across to a house on the other side, would you do it? I am sure you would – although you probably wouldn't much like doing it." **-Robert Baden-Powell**


"A soldier who has proper confidence in his own skill and strength entertains no thought of mutiny." **-Publius Flavius Vegetius Renatus**


"Arm yourselves, and be valiant men, and see that ye be in readiness against the morning, that ye may fight with these nations, that are assembled together against us to destroy us and our sanctuary. For it is better for us to die in battle, than to behold the calamities of our people and our sanctuary." **-Judas Maccabeus**


"They [the Romans] faced the rebellious slaves, aided though these were to some extent by the military training and discipline they had acquired from their Roman masters. This shows what a great advantage resolute courage is." **-Julius Caesar**


"I don't believe there is any man, who in his heart of hearts, wouldn't rather be called brave than have any other virtue attributed to him. And this elemental, if you like unreasoning, male attitude is a sound one, because courage is not merely a virtue; it is the virtue. Without it there are no other virtues. Faith, hope, charity, all the rest don't become virtues until it takes courage to exercise them. Courage is not only the basis of all virtue; it is its expression. True, you may be bad and brave, but you can't be good without being brave." **-Field Marshal Viscount Slim of Burma**

"Hidden valor is as bad as cowardice." -**Roman proverb**

"When I ask can war make any man a coward it is no answer to point to men who were cowards before they were soldiers. Such men went about wearing labels for all to read. From the first they were plainly unable to stand this test of men. They had about them the marks known to our calling of the incomplete man, the stamp of degeneracy. The whole miserable issue could have been foretold, the man was certain to crack when the strain came." -**Lord Moran**

"In the legion were two very brave centurions named Titus Pullo and Lucius Vorenus, both of them nearly qualified for the first grade. They were always disputing which was the better soldier and every year, the competition for promotion set them quarrelling. When the fighting [against the Gauls] was at its height, Pullo cried: 'Why hesitate, Vorenus? What better opportunity do you want to prove your courage? Today shall decide between us." -**Julius Caesar**

"If numbers are what matters, all Greece cannot match a small part of that army; but if courage is what counts, this number is sufficient."
-**Leonidas, before the battle of Thermopylae.**

"If one is sure of victory he will fight; if unsure he should not fight." -**Sun Bin**

"Men with no great confidence in themselves or in their horses are not ill-qualified to guard, or withdraw within shelter, the property of friends; since fear, as the proverb has it, makes a shrewd watchman." -**Xenophon**

"Courage is the first of the human qualities because it is the quality which guarantees all the others." -**Winston Churchill**

"As a rule, what is out of sight disturbs men's minds more seriously than what they see." **-Julius Caesar**

"Without courage, all other virtues lose their meaning." **-Winston Churchill**

"God grant me the courage not to give up what I think is right, even though I think it is hopeless." **-Fleet Admiral Chester W. Nimitz**

"This is courage ... to bear unflinchingly what heaven sends." **-Euripides**

"I am not afraid; I was born to do this." **-Joan of Arc**

"Let us never negotiate out of fear. But let us never fear to negotiate." **-John F. Kennedy**

"None but a coward dares to boast that he has never known fear." **-Ferdinand Foch**

"Be strong and of good courage." **-Motto of Joshua**

"Men are moved by two levers only: fear and self interest." **-Napoleon Bonaparte**

"The brave man inattentive to his duty, is worth little more to his country, than the coward who deserts her in the hour of danger." **-Andrew Jackson**

"Courage is endurance for one moment more…" **-Unknown Marine Second Lieutenant in Vietnam**

"The courage of the soldier is heightened by the knowledge of his profession."
|-**Publius Flavius Vegetius Renatus**

"But this noble capacity to rise above the most menacing dangers should also be considered as a principle in itself, separate and active. Indeed, in what field of human activity is boldness more at home than in war?

A soldier, whether drummer boy or general, possesses no nobler quality; it is the very metal that gives edge and luster to the sword." -**Karl von Clausewitz**

"War is the realm of danger; therefore courage is the soldier's first requirement. Courage is of two kinds: courage in the face of personal danger, and courage to accept responsibility, either before the tribunal of some outside power or before the court of one's own conscience." -**Karl von Clausewitz**

"Make peace a time of training for war, and battle an exhibition of bravery."
-**The Emperor Maurice**

"By cowardice I do not mean fear. Fear is the response of the instinct of self-preservation to danger. It is only morbid, as Aristotle taught, when it is out of proportion to the degree of danger. In invincible fear - 'fear stronger than I am' - the soldier has to struggle with a flood of emotions; he is made that way. But fear even when morbid is not cowardice. That is a label we reserve for something that a man does. What passes through his mind is his own affair." -**Lord Moran**

"There is, of course, such a thing as individual courage, which has a value in war, but familiarity with danger, experience in war and its common attendants, and personal habit, are equally valuable traits, and these are the qualities with which we usually have to deal in war. All men naturally shrink from pain and danger, and only incur their risk from some higher motive, or from habit; so that I would define true courage to be a perfect sensibility of the measure of danger, and a mental willingness to incur it, rather

than that insensibility to danger of which I have heard far more than I have seen. The most courageous men are generally unconscious of possessing the quality; therefore, when one professes it too openly, by words or bearing, there is reason to mistrust it. I would further illustrate my meaning by describing a man of true courage to be one who possesses all his faculties and senses perfectly when serious danger is actually present."
**-General Tecumseh Sherman**

"Without supplies no army is brave." **-Frederick the Great**

"They are surely to be esteemed the bravest spirits who, having the clearest sense of both the pains and pleasures of life, do not on that account shrink from danger." **-Thucydides**

"In other cities whenever a man shows himself to be a coward his only punishment is that he is called a coward... But in Sparta anyone would be ashamed to dine or to wrestle with a coward... In the streets he must get out of the way... he must support his unmarried sisters at home and explain to them why they are still spinsters, he must live without a wife at his fireside... he may not wander about comfortably acting like someone with a clean reputation or else he is beaten by his betters. I don't wonder that where such a load of dishonor burdens the coward death seems preferable instead of a dishonored and shameful life." **-Xenophon**

"When someone said: 'Leonidas, are you here like this, to run such a risk with a few men against many?', he replied: 'If you think that I should rely on numbers, then not even the whole of Greece is enough, since it is a small fraction of their horde; but if I am to rely on courage, then even this number is quite adequate.'" **-King Leonidas of Sparta**

"Boldness governed by superior intellect is the mark of a hero. This kind of boldness does not consist in defying the natural order of things and in crudely offending the laws of probability; it is rather a matter of energetically support-ing that higher form of analysis by which genius arrives at a decision: rapid, only partly conscious weighing of the possibilities. Boldness can lend wings to intellect and insight; the stronger the wings then, the greater the heights, the wider the view, and the better results; though a greater prize, of course, involves greater risks." -**Karl von Clausewitz**

"A pursuit gives even cowards confidence." -**Xenophon**

"Determination in a single instance is an expression of courage; if it becomes characteristic, a mental habit. But here we are referring not to physical courage but to the courage to accept responsi-bility, a courage in the face of moral danger. This has often been called courage d'esprit, because it is created by the intellect. That, however, does not make it an act of the intellect: it is an act of temperament. Intelligence alone is not courage; we often see that the most intelligent people are irresolute. Since in the rush of events a man is governed by feelings rather than by thought, the intellect needs to arouse the quality of courage, which then supports and sustains it in action.

Looked at in this way, the role of determination is to limit the agonies of doubt and the perils of hesitation when the motives for action are inadequate..." -**Karl von Clausewitz**

"Why, you may take the most gallant sailor, the most intrepid airman, or the most audacious soldier, put them at a table together - what do you get? The sum total of their fears." -**Winston Churchill**

"Never take counsel of your fears." -**Stonewall Jackson**

"My troops are good and well-disciplined, and the most important thing of all is that I have thoroughly habituated them to perform everything that they are required to execute. You will do something more easily, to a higher standard, and more bravely when you know that you will do it well." -**Frederick the Great**

"Fatigue makes cowards of us all." -**General Patton**

"War is not at all such a difficult art as people think…In reality it would seem that he is vanquished who is afraid of his adversary and that the whole secret of war is this."
**-Napoleon Bonaparte**


"Each man must think not only of himself, but think of his buddy fighting beside him. We don't want yellow cowards in this army, to send back to the States after the war and breed more like them. The brave men will breed brave men. One of the bravest men I saw in the African campaign was one of the fellows I saw on top of a telegraph pole in the midst of furious fire while we were plowing towards Tunis. I stopped and asked him what in the hell he was doing there at a time like that. He answered, 'Fixing the wire, sir.' Isn't it a little unhealthy right now, I asked. 'Yes sir, but this God damn wire has got to be fixed.'" **-General Patton**


"It doesn't take a hero to order men into battle. It takes a hero to be one of those men who goes into battle." **-General Norman Schwarzkopf**


"The ugly truth is revealed that fear is the foundation of obedience."
**-Winston Churchill**


"Go forward bravely. Fear nothing. If you will go forward like a man, you shall have your whole Kingdom!" **-Joan of Arc to King Charles VII.**

# Chapter 2
# Leadership

*O*ne of the distinctive marks of any armed force is its hierarchy – its system of ranking. All warriors need to follow leaders, and in turn, these leaders will make or break a fighting force. But the role of the leader has changed from what it used to be – modern day generals are no longer expected to lead the charge in every battle – but the responsibility of leadership has not changed. A leader of a military unit has total command – and also has total responsibility. And today, as always, leaders have to inspire and encourage those they lead.

*Of course, in days gone by, it was fighting ability that created kings. "We will have a king over us… that our king may judge us and go out before us and fight our battles."*

*The head of state was the head of the army, and it was no coincidence that the tokens of royalty – crowns and scepters – were decorated versions of fighting gear (helmets and war-clubs or spears) as leadership took on the dual responsibility of leading both a nation and its army.*

---

"Now as for me, my men, there is not one of you who has not with his own eyes seen me strike a blow in battle; I have watched and witnessed your valour in the field, and your acts of courage I know by heart, with every detail of when and where they took place: and this, surely, is not a thing of small importance. I was your pupil before I was your commander; I shall advance into the line with soldiers I have a thousand times praised and rewarded; and the enemy we shall meet are raw troops with a raw general, neither knowing anything of the other." **-Hannibal**


"Soldiers must be treated in the first instance with humanity, but kept under control by means of iron discipline. This is a certain road to victory." **-Sun Tzu**

"You must endeavour to make your practice correspond with what you preach."
**-Xenophon**


"The general must be first in the toils and fatigues of the army. In the heat of summer he does not spread his parasol, nor in the cold of winter don thick clothing... He waits until the army's wells have been dug and only then drinks; until the army's food is cooked before he eats; until the army's fortifications have been completed, to shelter himself."
**-Sun Tzu**


"When someone can exercise sole control over the army, without being governed by other men, he is a military weapon." **-Jiang Taigong**


"It doesn't take a hero to order men into battle. It takes a hero to be one of those men who goes into battle." **-General Norman Schwarzkopf**


"When placed in command - take charge." **-General Norman Schwarzkopf**


"His [the general's] business, so at least it seems to me, will be to keep his men perpetually in readiness to strike a blow, and without exposing himself, to play sentinel, waiting for any false move on the part of the hostile armament."
**-Xenophon**


"In the election of kings they have regard to birth; in that of generals, to valor. Their kings have not an absolute or unlimited power; and their generals command less through the force of authority, than of example. If they are daring, adventurous, and conspicuous in action, they procure obedience from the admiration they inspire." **-Tacitus, on the Germanic warriors.**


"Teach them, then, and show them without being angry." **-Marcus Aurelius**

"There are five dangerous faults which may affect a general:

(1) Recklessness, which leads to destruction;

(2) Cowardice, which leads to capture;

(3) A hasty temper, which can be provoked by insults;

(4) A delicacy of honor which is sensitive to shame;

(5) Over-solicitude for his men, which exposes him to worry and trouble.

These are the five besetting sins of a general, ruinous to the conduct of war. When an army is overthrown and its leader slain, the cause will surely be found among these five dangerous faults. Let them be a subject of meditation." -**Sun Tzu**

"Pay heed to nourishing the troops; do not unnecessarily fatigue them. Unite them in spirit; conserve their strength. Make unfathomable plans for the movement of the army. Thus, such troops need no encouragement to be vigilant. Without extorting their support the general obtains it; without inviting their affection he gains it; without demanding their trust he wins it." -**Sun Tzu**

"The commander-in-chief focuses on winning the minds of the capable, remunerate the meritorious, and having his will adopted by the masses. Thus if he has the same wishes as the masses, there is nothing he cannot accomplish." -**Huang Shi Gong**

"He [the Praetor or commander of a legion] ought to be a careful and diligent officer, as the sole charge of forming the legion to regularity and obedience depended on him and the excellence of the soldiers redounded entirely to his own honor and credit."
-**Publius Flavius Vegetius Renatus**

"You must contrive to make your men amenable to discipline, without which neither good horses, nor a firm seat, nor splendour of equipment will be of any use at all."
-**Xenophon**

"Leadership is a potent combination of strategy and character. But if you must be without one, be without the strategy." -**General Norman Schwarzkopf**

"If the general is not benevolent, then the army will not be close to or support him. If the general is not courageous, then the army will not be fierce. If the general is not wise, then the army will be in doubts. If the general is not perspicacious, then the army will be confounded. If the general is not quick-witted and acute, then the army will lose the opportunity. If the general is not constantly alert, the army will be weak in defense. If the general is not strong and forceful, then the army will fail in their duty. Thus the general is the Master of Fate. The army is ordered because of him, and they are disordered because of him as well. If one obtains someone who is worthy to serve as general, the army will be strong and the state will prosper. If one does not obtain a worthy as general, the army will be weak and state will perish." **-Jiang Taigong**

"An officer must be competent to so assert himself in speech or action so that those under him will no longer hesitate. They will recognise of themselves that it is a good thing and a right to obey, to follow their leader, to rush to close quarters with the foe. A desire will consume them to achieve some deed of glory and renown. A capacity will be given them patiently to abide by the resolution of their souls." **-Xenophon**

"The commander-in-chief should make changes and not be constant when situation depicts. He should change and transform in response to the enemy. He does not precede affairs; when the enemy moves, he immediately follows up with it. Thus he is able to formulate inexhaustible strategies and methods of control to secure victory, sustain his gains, bring tranquility and order to the whole land, and settle the Nine Barbarians. Such strategist is a teacher for an emperor." **-Huang Shi Gong**

"Dependability, integrity, the characteristic of never knowingly doing anything wrong, that you would never cheat anyone, that you would give everybody a fair deal. Character is a sort of an all-inclusive thing. If a man has character, everyone has confidence in him. Soldiers must have confidence in their leader." **-Omar Bradley**

"When the army is mobilized and advances into the field, the sole authority lies with the general." **-Huang Shi Gong**

"Courage is but one of the many required characteristics of a general. Being only courageous, one would rashly rush into battle without any consideration for the gains and loss. Such action is not acceptable." **-Wu Qi**

"Again, if there is prospect of danger on the march, a prudent general can hardly show his wisdom better than by sending out advanced patrols in front of the ordinary exploring parties to reconnoitre every inch of ground minutely... These are precepts known, I admit, to nearly all the world, but it is by no means every one who will take pains to apply them carefully." **-Xenophon**

"A competent leader can get efficient service from poor troops, while on the contrary an incapable leader can demoralize the best of troops." **-John Pershing**

"If the leader of the army and commander of the masses does not first establish his plans, the proper equipment will not be prepared. If his instructions are not precise and trusted, the officers and men will not be trained. Under such conditions, they cannot comprise a conqueror's army." **-Jiang Taigong**

"Lead from the front." **-Audie Murphy**

"In order to create a spirit of obedience in your subordinates, you have two formidable instruments; as a matter of plain reason you can show them what a host of blessings the word discipline implies; and as a matter of hard fact you can, within the limits of the law, enable the well-disciplined to reap advantage, while the undisciplined are made to feel the pinch at every turn." **-Xenophon**

"The general of cavalry, as patron of the whole department, is naturally responsible for its efficient working. In view, however, of the task imposed upon that officer had he to carry out these various details single-handed, the state has chosen to associate with him certain coadjutors in the persons of the phylarchs (or tribal captains), and has besides imposed upon the senate a share in the superintendence of the cavalry. This being so, two things appear to me desirable; the first is, so to work upon the phylarch that he shall share your own enthusiasm for the honour of the corps; and secondly, to have at your disposal in the senate able orators, whose language may instil a wholesome fear into the knights themselves, and thereby make them all the better men, or tend to pacify the senate on occasion and disarm unseasonable anger." -**Xenophon**

"A sovereign of high character and intelligence must be able to know the right man, should place the responsibility on him, and expect results." -**Sun Tzu**

"It is the duty of a good general to have every corps instructed separately in every part of the drill by tribunes of known capacity chosen for that purpose. He should afterwards form them into one body and train them in all the maneuvers of the line as for a general action. He must frequently drill them himself to try their skill and strength, and to see whether they perform their evolutions with proper regularity and are sufficiently attentive to the sound of the trumpets, the motions of the colors and to his own orders and signals. If deficient in any of these particulars, they must be instructed and exercised till perfect." -**Publius Flavius Vegetius Renatus**

"Obedience to lawful authority is the foundation of manly character."
-**Robert E. Lee**

"In the armies, and among every ten men, there must be one of more life, of more heart, or at least of more authority, who with his spirit, with his words, and with his example keeps the others firm and disposed to fight." -**Machiavelli**

"If the general is not brave, his officers and men will be terrified. If the general moves the army recklessly, the army will not be imposing. If his anger implicates the innocent, the whole army will be in fear." -**Huang Shi Gong**

"But for a soldier his duty is plain. He is to obey the orders of all those placed over him and whip the enemy wherever he meets him." -**Ulysses S. Grant**

"Leadership is intangible, and therefore no weapon ever designed can replace it."
-**Omar Bradley**

"Another excellent specimen of inventiveness may be seen in the general's ability, while holding a weak position himself, to conjure up so lively an apprehension in the enemy that he will not dream of attacking; or conversely, when, being in a strong position himself, he can engender a fatal boldness in the adversary to venture an attack. Thus with the least cost to yourself, you will best be able to catch your enemy tripping."
-**Xenophon**

"As to your lieutenant, it is every way important to appoint a good man to this post, whose bravery will tell; and in case of need at any time to charge the enemy, the cheering accents of his voice will infuse strength into those in front; or when the critical moment of retreat arrives, his sage conduct in retiring will go far, we may well conclude, towards saving his division." -**Xenophon**

"If you would stir in each [officer] a personal ambition to appear at the head of his own squadron in all ways splendidly appointed, the best incentive will be your personal example." -**Xenophon**

"What measures will ensure the soldiers will be victorious? Control is foremost."
-**Wu Qi**

"Now those who command the army must share joy and sorrow with the officers and men, and confront safety and danger with them. Only then can they confront the enemy, gained full victory and the enemy completely destroyed." -**Huang Shi Gong**

"A true leader has the confidence to stand alone, the courage to make tough decisions, and the compassion to listen to the needs of others. He does not set out to be a leader, but becomes one by the equality of his actions and the integrity of his intent." **-Douglas MacArthur**

"Whenever one mobilizes the army, the commanding general should be the one giving orders. He must have an understanding of all aspects, not depending on one technique alone." **-Jiang Taigong**

"What am I lying here for? ...So far from anybody bothering to take any stops for our defense, we are lying here as though we had a chance of enjoying a quiet time. What city, then, do I expect will produce the general to take the right steps? Am I waiting until I become a little older? I shall never be any older at all if I hand myself over to the enemy today." **-Xenophon**

"Thus a vigilant and prudent general will carefully weigh in his council the state of his own forces and of those of the enemy, just as a civil magistrate judging between two contending parties. If he finds himself in many respects superior to his adversary, he must by no means defer bringing on an engagement. But if he knows himself inferior, he must avoid general actions and endeavor to succeed by surprises, ambuscades and stratagems. These, when skillfully managed by good generals, have often given them the victory over enemies superior both in numbers and strength."
**-Publius Flavius Vegetius Renatus**

"After all, you are generals, you are officers and captains. In peace time, you got more pay and respect than they did. Now, in war time, you ought to hold yourselves to be braver than the general mass of men, and to take decisions for the rest, and, if necessary, to be the first to do the hard work." **-Xenophon.**

"A general is just as good or just as bad as the troops under his command make him."
**-Douglas MacArthur**


"A commander-in-chief therefore, whose power and dignity are so great and to whose fidelity and bravery the fortunes of his countrymen, the defense of their cities, the lives of the soldiers, and the glory of the state, are entrusted, should not only consult the good of the army in general, but extend his care to every private soldier in it."
**-Publius Flavius Vegetius Renatus**


"Where there is no-one in control, nothing useful or distinguished can ever get done."
**-Xenophon**


"I am not afraid of an army of lions led by a sheep; I am afraid of an army of sheep led by a lion." **-Alexander the Great**


"The essence of governing the state and army lies in understanding the needs of the people and managing the affairs of the state.  Protect those that are in danger; bring happiness to those who are in fear; forgive and ask for the return of those who rebel; give justice to those that have been wronged; investigate all grievances that are submitted to you; raise up the lowly; suppress those that are strong and arrogant... get close to good strategists; stay away from slanderers; check all negative comments; eliminate the rebellious; stifle those that act willfully; diminish the arrogant; summon and use those that turn their allegiance to you; settle those that submit to you; release those who surrender." **-Huang Shi Gong's techniques for managing people.**


"When soldiers have been baptized in the fire of a battlefield, they have all one rank in my eyes." **-Napoleon Bonaparte**


"I can no longer obey; I have tasted command, and I cannot give it up."
**-Napoleon Bonaparte**

"The general who advances without coveting fame and retreats without fearing disgrace, whose only thought is to protect his country and do good service for his sovereign, is the jewel of the kingdom." -**Sun Tzu**

"The true general must be able to take in, deceive, decoy, delude his adversary at every turn, as the particular occasion demands. In fact, there is no instrument of war more cunning than chicanery; which is not surprising when one reflects that even little boys, when playing, "How many (marbles) have I got in my hand?" are able to take one another in successfully. Out goes a clenched fist, but with such cunning that he who holds a few is thought to hold several; or he may present several and appear to be holding only a few. Is it likely that a grown man, giving his whole mind to methods of chicanery, will fail of similar inventiveness? Indeed, when one comes to consider what is meant by advantages snatched in war, one will find, i think, that the greater part of them, and those the more important, must be attributed in some way or other to displays of craft; which things being so, a man had better either not attempt to exercise command, or, as part and parcel of his general equipment, let him pray to Heaven to enable him to exercise this faculty and be at pains himself to cultivate his own inventiveness."
-**Xenophon**

"Indeed, I take it to be the mark of a really prudent general never to run a risk of his own choosing, except where it is plain to him beforehand, that he will get the better of his adversary. To play into the enemy's hands may more fitly be described as treason to one's fellow-combatants than true manliness." -**Xenophon**

"I do not believe in the proverb that in order to be able to command one must know how to obey... Insubordination may only be the evidence of a strong mind."
-**Napoleon Bonaparte**

"Power is my mistress. I have worked too hard at her conquest to allow anyone to take her away from me." -**Napoleon Bonaparte**

"I have only one counsel for you – be master." -**Napoleon Bonaparte**

"The greatest general is he who makes the fewest mistakes." -**Napoleon Bonaparte**

"A leader is a dealer of hope." -**Napoleon Bonaparte**

"You should make your commands clear and be careful about your orders."
-**Jiang Taigong**

"Conquering the world on horseback is easy; it is dismounting and governing that is hard." -**Genghis Khan**

"One man who has been trained in warfare can instruct ten men. Ten men who have been trained can train a hundred men. A hundred men who have been trained can train a thousand men. A thousand men who have been trained can train ten thousand men. Ten thousand men who have been trained can train the whole army." -**Wu Qi**

"I love power. But it is as an artist that I love it. I love it as a musician loves his violin, to draw out its sounds and chords and harmonies." -**Napoleon Bonaparte**

"What we refer to the five important characteristics [of a general] are courage, wisdom, benevolence, trustworthiness and loyalty. If he is courageous, he cannot be overwhelmed. If he is wise, he cannot be forced into turmoil. If he is benevolent, he will love his men. If he is trustworthy, he will not be deceitful. If he is loyal, he will always have interest on the state.  What are referred to as the ten flawed characters are as follows: being courageous and treating death lightly; being hasty and impatient; being greedy and lust for gains; being benevolent but unable to inflict suffering; being wise but afraid; being trustworthy and liking to trust others; being unscrupulous and incorruptible but not loving men; being wise but indecisive; being resolute and self-reliant; being fearful and very dependent on people." -**Jiang Taigong**

"Thus the wise general does not rescind an order. Rewards and punishment must be carried out, much like how Heaven and Earth work, without fail. Only then the general can employ the men. When the officers and soldiers follow orders, the army can then be deployed." -**Huang Shi Gong**

"The consummate leader cultivates the moral law, and strictly adheres to method and discipline; thus it is in his power to control success." -**Sun Tzu**

"There are certain things in war of which the commander alone comprehends the importance. Nothing but his superior firmness and ability can subdue and surmount all difficulties." -**Napoleon Bonaparte**

"Do not, because you are honored, regard other men as lowly." -**Jiang Taigong**

"I am a soldier, I fight where I am told, and I win where I fight." -**General Patton**

"Lead me, follow me, or get out of my way." -**General Patton**

"War is very simple, direct, and ruthless. It takes a simple, direct, and ruthless man to wage war." -**General Patton**

"If the leader is filled with high ambition and if he pursues his aims with audacity and strength of will, he will reach them in spite of all obstacles." -**Karl von Clausewitz**

"The general shares heat and cold, labor and suffering, hunger and satiety with the officers and men. Therefore, when the soldiers hear the sound of the drum, they are happy, and when they hear the sound of the gong, they are angry. When attacking at high wall or crossing a deep lake, under a hail of arrows and stones, the officers will compete to be the first to scale the wall. When the blades clash, the officers will compete to be the first to go forward. It is not because they like death and take pleasure in being wounded, but because the general knows their feelings of heat and cold, hunger and satiety, and clearly displays his knowledge of their labor and suffering." **-Jiang Taigong**

"Treat the people as they should be treated shows the greatness of the ruler."
**-Huang Shi Gong**

"Dictators ride to and fro upon tigers which they dare not dismount. And the tigers are getting hungry." **-Winston Churchill**

"Humility must always be the portion of any man who receives acclaim earned in the blood of his followers and the sacrifices of his friends."
**-Dwight D. Eisenhower**

"Courage which goes against military expediency is stupidity, or, if it is insisted upon by a commander, irresponsibility." **-Erwin Rommel**

"Never forget that no military leader has ever become great without audacity. If the leader is filled with high ambition and if he pursues his aims with audacity and strength of will, he will reach them in spite of all obstacles." **-Karl von Clausewitz**

"The one who unifies the army and gains control of the situation is the general, while the ones that bring about conquest and defeat the enemy are the men, the army. Thus a general that is not able to manage and control an army should not lead his troops, and a rebellious army should not be used against an enemy." **-Huang Shi Gong**

"He was a tall man with the body of a giant, cheerful in appearance with agreeable features… but with a wild look… a most spirited fighting man, with all his limbs very strong and firm. He was most liberal in all his gifts, very fair in his judgments, most compassionate in comforting the sad, a most skilful counselor, very patient when suffering, a distinguished speaker, who above all hunted down falsehood and deceit and treachery." -**Description of William Wallace**

"The King daily and nightly in his own person visited and searched the watches, orders and stations of every part of his host, and whom he found diligent, he praised and thanked; and the negligent, he corrected and chastised." -**Description of Henry V**

"I would rather have a plain russet-coated captain that knows what he fights for, and loves what he knows, than which you call a 'gentleman' and nothing else."
-**Oliver Cromwell**

"It is thus justice (one would have to say) which must be the main responsibility of a sovereign. Since it is the prime interest of the many people whom they control, they must give it priority over any other interest of their own." -**Frederick the Great**

"I believe that a general who receives good advice from a subordinate officer should profit by it. Any patriotic servant of the state should forget himself when in that service, and look only to the interests of the state. In particular, he must not let the source of an idea influence him. Ideas of others can be as valuable as his own and should be judged only by the results they are likely to produce." -**Frederick the Great**

"The situation was saved by two things – first, the knowledge and experience of the soldiers, whose training in earlier battles enabled them to decide for themselves what needed doing, without waiting to be told; secondly, the order which Caesar had issued to all his generals, not to leave the work but to stay each with his own legion... As the enemy was so close and advancing so swiftly, the generals did not wait for further orders but on their own responsibility took the measures they thought proper." -**Julius Caesar**

"[The general's] reputation, virtues, benevolence and courage must be respected by his subordinates and calm the masses." -**Wu Qi**

"A great prince must take control of his troops, to remain in his army as if it were his residence; his interests, duty and glory, all hinge on the outcome here. Just as he is the head of distributive justice, he is also the guard and the defender of his people; he must treat the defense of his subjects as his most important ministry, which he must for this reason entrust only to himself. His interests also necessitate going to the field with his army, since his person is required: then the consulting and the execution are followed with an extreme speed. Beside, his presence puts an end to the disagreements of his generals, so disastrous to the armies and so contrary to the interest of the Master; it also puts the prince in command of the logistics, the ammunition and the war supplies, without which even Caesar himself at the head of one hundred thousand combatants would be nothing, ever." -**Frederick the Great**

"I am up and about when I am ill, and in the most appalling weather. I am on horseback when other men would be flat out on their beds, complaining. We are made for action, and activity is the sovereign remedy for all physical ills." -**Frederick the Great**

"A good and wise king was never dethroned in England, even by large armies, and all its bad kings succumbed to 'usurpers' who begin their campaign with four thousand regular troops. There is no gain by being malicious with misanthropes, but there is by being virtuous and intrepid with them; you will make your people virtuous like you, neighbors will want to imitate you, and the humanity-haters will scramble from the light." -**Frederick the Great**

"The suggestion that the men would not obey orders to advance did not trouble him at all; for he knew that in all cases in which an army had refused obedience, it was either because their generals had been unsuccessful and were regarded as unlucky, or because they were proven dishonest by the discovery of some misconduct. His [Caesar's] own integrity was attested by his whole life; his power of commanding success, by the campaign against the Helvetii. Therefore, he was going to do that very night what he had at first intended to defer until later: he would move camp in the early hours of the morning, so as to find out with the least possible delay whether their sense of honour and duty or their fear was the stronger. If no one else would follow him, he would go all the same, accompanied only by the 10th legion; of its loyalty, he had no doubt, and it would serve him as his bodyguard." -**Julius Caesar**

"An army of lions commanded by a deer will never be an army of lions."
-**Napoleon Bonaparte**

"If the general leads the men in person, the soldiers will become the most valiant under Heaven." -**Huang Shi Gong**

"For ever I see him high on horseback, the eternal eyes set in the marble of that imperial visage, looking on with the calm of destiny at his Guards as they march past… the old grenadiers glanced up at him with so awesome a devotion, so sympathetic an earnestness, with the pride of death."
-**Description of Napoleon by poet Heinrich Heine.**

"The control and management of army's movement lies in the hand of one general. That is the vital point for morale." -**Wu Qi**

"I have served, commanded, conquered forty years. I have seen the destiny of the world in my hands, and I have known that at every turn, the fate of States hinges on a single moment." -**Napoleon, echoing a passage by the writer Voltaire.**

"He [the general] must also, as it appears to me, be capable of great physical endurance; since clearly, if he has to run full tilt against an armament present, as we picture, in such force that not even our whole state cares to cope with it, it is plain he must accept whatever fate is due, where might is right, himself unable to retaliate." -**Xenophon**

"The officer will need perpetually to act as circumstances require. He must take in the situation at a glance, and carry out unflinchingly whatever is expedient for the moment. To set down in writing everything that he must do, is not a whit more possible than to know the future as a whole. But of all hints and suggestions the most important to my mind is this: whatever you determine to be right, with diligence endeavour to perform. For be it tillage of the soil, or trading, or seafaring, or the art of ruling, without pains applied to bring the matter to perfection, the best theories in the world, the most correct conclusions, will be fruitless." -**Xenophon**

"Men must be habituated to obey or they cannot be controlled in battle and the neglect of the least important order impairs the proper influence of the officer." -**Robert E. Lee**

"Indeed, to put the matter in a nutshell, there is small risk a general will be regarded with contempt by those he leads, if, whatever he may have to preach, he shows himself best able to perform." -**Xenophon**

"Good-morning; good-morning!" the General said.
When we met him last week on our way to the line.
Now the soldiers he smiled at are most of 'em dead,
And we're cursing his staff for incompetent swine.
'He's a cheery old card,' grunted Harry to Jack.
As they slogged up to Arras with rifle and pack.
But he did for them both by his plan of attack." -**Siegfried Sassoon**

"Be cautious in commanding the army; do not allow the enemy to know your true situation." -**Jiang Taigong**

"He [Caesar] went on to say the those who tried to disguise their own cowardice by pretending to be anxious about the corn-supply or the difficulties of the route were

acting presumptuously: it was plain that they either lacked confidence in their general's sense of duty or else meant to dictate to him.  He was attending to these matters."
**-Julius Caesar**


"It is possible for a general with a head on his shoulders to hang on the heels of an enemy in security, and to determine with precision the exact number of the enemy he will care to deal with." **-Xenophon**


"If you are indulgent, but unable to make your authority felt; kind-hearted, but unable to enforce your commands; and incapable, moreover, of quelling disorder, your soldiers are like spoilt children: they are useless for any practical purpose." **-Sun Tzu**


"Our army has always had two policies. First, we must be ruthless to our enemies, we must overpower and annihilate them. Second, we must be kind to our own, to the people, to our comrades and to our superiors and subordinates, and unite with them."
**-Mao Zedong**


"If thou art able, correct by teaching those who do wrong; but if thou canst not, remember that indulgence is given to thee for this purpose. And the gods, too, are indulgent to such persons; and for some purposes they even help them to get health, wealth, reputation; so kind they are. And it is in thy power also." **-Marcus Aurelius**


"Thus the good general, in nurturing his officers, treats them no differently than himself. Thus he is able to unite everyone and gain complete victory." **-Huang Shi Gong**


"To accept command without declining, destroy the enemy and only afterward speak about returning is the proper form of behavior for a general. Thus when the army goes forth, his only thought is to die with glory then to live with shame." **-Wu Qi**

"There is no command without leadership." -**Sun Bin**

"If, further, the men shall see in their commander one who, with the knowledge how to act, has force of will and cunning to make them get the better of the enemy; and if, further, they have got the notion well into their heads that this same leader may be trusted not to lead them recklessly against the foe, without the help of Heaven, or despite the auspices – I say, you have a list of virtues which will make those under his command the more obedient to their ruler." -**Xenophon**

"One final aspect of leadership is the frequent necessity to be a philosopher, able to understand and to explain the lack of a moral economy in this universe, for many people have a great deal of difficulty with the fact that virtue is not always rewarded nor is evil always punished. To handle tragedy may indeed be the mark of an educated man, for one of the principal goals of education is to prepare us for failure. To say that is not to encourage resignation to the whims of fate, but to acknowledge the need for forethought about how to cope with undeserved reverses. It's important that our leadership steel themselves against the natural reaction of lashing out or withdrawing when it happens. The test of character is not 'hanging in there' when the light at the end of the tunnel is expected but performance of duty and persistence of example when the situation rules out the possibility of the light ever coming." -**Admiral James B. Stockdale**

"When on active service, the commander must prove himself conspicuously careful in the matter of forage, quarters, water-supply, outposts, and all other requisites; forecasting the future and keeping ever a wakeful eye in the interest of those under him; and in case of any advantage won, the truest gain which the head of affairs can reap is to share with his men the profits of success." -**Xenophon**

"Leadership is understanding people and involving them to help you do a job. That takes all of the good characteristics, like integrity, dedication of purpose, selflessness, knowledge, skill, implacability, as well as determination not to accept failure."
-**Admiral Arleigh A. Burke**

"I have developed almost an obsession as to the certainty with which you can judge a division, or any other large unit, merely by knowing its commander intimately. Of course, we have had pounded into us all through our school courses that the exact level of a commander's personality and ability is always reflected in his unit - but I did not realize, until opportunity came for comparisons on a rather large scale, how infallibly the commander and unit are almost one and the same thing." **-Dwight D. Eisenhower**

"Generals ought to be given advice, in the first place from men of foresight, the experts who have specialized in military affairs, and who have learned from experience; secondly, from those who are on the spot, who see the terrain, who know the enemy, who can judge the right moment for action, who are, as it were, shipmates sharing the same danger. Therefore, if there is anyone who is confident that he can advise me about the best interest of the nation in the campaign which I am now about to conduct, let him not deny the state his services - let him come with me to Macedonia. I will assist him by providing his passage, his horse, his tent, yes, and his travelling money. If anyone finds this prospect too irksome, and prefers the ease of the city to the hardships of campaign, let him not steer the ship from his place on shore." **-Lucius Aemilius Paulus**

"People ask the difference between a leader and a boss. . . The leader works in the open, and the boss in covert. The leader leads, and the boss drives." **-Theodore Roosevelt**

"Leadership and learning are indispensable to each other." **-John F. Kennedy**

"A few men had the stuff of leadership in them, they were like rafts to which all the rest of humanity clung for support and hope." **-Lord Moran**

"There is nothing like seeing the other fellow run to bring back your courage."
**-Field Marshal Viscount Slim of Burma**

"There is required for the composition of a great commander not only massive common sense and reasoning power, not only imagination, but also an element of legerdemain, an original and sinister touch, which leaves the enemy puzzled as well as beaten."
**-Winston Churchill**

"No matter what may be the ability of the officer, if he loses the confidence of his troops, disaster must sooner or later ensue." **-Robert E. Lee**

"The company is the true unit of discipline, and the captain is the company. A good captain makes a good company, and he should have the power to reward as well as punish. The fact that soldiers would naturally like to have a good fellow for their captain is the best reason why he should be appointed by the colonel, or by some superior authority, instead of being elected by the men." **-General Tecumseh Sherman**

"We are not interested in generals who win victories without bloodshed. The fact that slaughter is a horrifying spectacle must make us take war more seriously, but not provide an excuse for gradually blunting our swords in the name of humanity. Sooner or later someone will come along with a sharp sword and hack off our arms."
**-Karl von Clausewitz**

"Being responsible sometimes means pissing people off." **-Colin Powell**

"The true way to be popular with the troops is not to be free and familiar with them, but to make them believe you know more than they do." **-General Tecumseh Sherman**

"In the British Army there are no good units and no bad units - only good and bad officers and NCOs. They make or break the unit. Today we cannot afford anything but the good ones. No man can be given a more honourable task than to lead his fellow countrymen in war. We, the officers and NCOs, owe it to the men we command and to our country that we make ourselves fit to lead the best soldiers in the world, that in peace the training we give them is practical, alive and purposeful, and that in war our leadership is wise, resolute and unselfish.

Leaders are made more often than they are born. You all have leadership in you. Develop it by thought, by training and by practice..." **-Field Marshal Viscount Slim of Burma**

"A prince should therefore have no other aim or thought, nor take up any other thing for his study, but war and its organization and discipline, for that is the only art that is necessary to one who commands, and it is of such virtue that it not only maintains those who are born princes, but often enables men of private fortune to attain to that rank." **-Machiavelli**

"Victory and disaster establish indestructable bonds between armies and their commanders." **-Napoleon Bonaparte**

"There is a gift of being able to see at a glance the possibilities offered by the terrain... One can call it the coup d'oeil and it is inborn in great generals." **-Napoleon Bonaparte**

"Nothing is easy in war. Mistakes are always paid for in casualties and troops are quick to sense any blunder made by their commanders." **-Dwight D. Eisenhower**"

Master Sun said: The traits of the true commander are: wisdom, humanity, respect, integrity, courage, and dignity. With his wisdom he humbles the enemy, with his humanity he draws the people near to him, with his respect he recruits men of talent and character, with his integrity he makes good on his rewards, with his courage he raises the morale of the men, and with his dignity he unifies his command. Thus, if he humbles his enemy, he is able to take advantage of changing circumstances; if the people are close to him, they will be of a mind to go to battle in earnest; if he employs men of talent and wisdom, his secret plans will work; if his rewards and punishments are invariably honored, his men will give their all; if the morale and courage of his troops is heightened, they will of themselves be increasingly martial and intimidating; if his command is unified, the men will serve their commander alone." -**Sun Tzu**

"The expert at battle seeks his victory from strategic advantage and does not demand it from his men. He is thus able to select the right men and exploit the strategic advantage. He who exploits the strategic advantage sends his men into battle like rolling logs and boulders. It is the nature of logs and boulders that on flat ground, they are stationary, but on steep ground, they roll; the square in shape tends to stop but the round tends to roll. Thus, that the strategic advantage of the expert commander in exploiting his men in battle can be likened to rolling round boulders down a steep ravine thousands of feet high says something about his strategic advantage." -**Sun Tzu**

"Is it really true that a seven-mile cross-country run is enforced upon all in this division, from generals to privates? ...It looks to me rather excessive. A colonel or a general ought not to exhaust himself in trying to compete with young boys running across country seven miles at a time. The duty of officers is no doubt to keep themselves fit, but still more to think of their men, and to take decisions affecting their safety or comfort. Who is the general of this division, and does he run the seven miles himself? If so, he may be more useful for football than for war. Could Napoleon have run seven miles across country at Austerlitz? Perhaps it was the other fellow he made run. In my experience, based on many years' observation, officers with high athletic qualifications are not usually successful in the higher ranks." -**Winston Churchill**

"If you wish to be loved by your soldiers, husband their blood and do not lead them to slaughter." -**Frederick the Great**

"A commander should have a profound understanding of human nature, the knack of smoothing out troubles, the power of winning affection while communicating energy, and the capacity for ruthless determination where required by circumstances. He needs

to generate an electrifying current, and to keep a cool head in applying it."
**-Captain Sir Basil Liddell Hart**


"A vital faculty of generalship is the power of grasping instantly the picture of the ground and the situation, of relating the one to the other, and the local to the general. It is that flair which makes the great executant." **-Captain Sir Basil Liddell Hart**


"A good general not only sees the way to victory; he also knows when victory is not possible." **-Polybius**


"Commanders must be just; if they are not just, they will lack dignity. If they lack dignity, they will lack charisma; and if they lack charisma, their soldiers will not face death for them. Therefore justice is the head of warriorship." **-Sun Bin**


"The leader must himself believe that willing obedience always beats forced obedience, and that he can get this only by really knowing what should be done. Thus he can secure obedience from his men because he can convince them that he knows best, precisely as a good doctor makes his patients obey him. Also he must be ready to suffer more hardships than he asks of his soldiers, more fatigue, greater extremities of cold and heat." **-Xenophon**


"What do we do with a man who refuses to accept either good fortune or bad? This is the only general who gives his enemy no rest when he is victorious, nor takes any himself when he is defeated. We shall never have done with fighting him, it seems, because he attacks out of confidence when he is winning, and out of shame when he is beaten."
**-Hannibal**

# Chapter 3
# Loyalty

*T*he bond between members of a fighting force is one of the strongest known to humanity. Members of a combat unit create the equivalency of family. What is one of the most used appellations for one's fellow soldiers: "brothers in arms." When lives are on the line, being able to trust and rely on those around you is crucial – and they have to be able to trust and rely on you. In these situations, selfishness begins the downfall of a fighting unit.

*Loyalty can also inspire a man or woman to take up arms and fight. How many armies were made up of people whose families and neighbors were threatened? Leaders of old knew that people will fight more bravely for what they know and love, and that the bonds within a unit will be forged more rapidly if other ties – the ties of a kindred neighborhood are forged. This was why Wu Qi recommended keeping people from the same village together in a unit, rather than separating them, and also why the old Anglo-Saxon and Celtic rulers kept their units together even in peacetime: the fighters were the "men of his household," often literally living under the same roof and continually strengthening the bonds of loyalty between them.*

---

"My first wish would be that my military family, and the whole Army, should consider themselves as a band of brothers, willing and ready to die for each other."
**-George Washington**


"Who fights only by himself is weak; who does it jointly is strong."
**-Frederick the Great**


"Men exist for the sake of one another. Teach them then or bear with them."
**-Marcus Aurelius**

"I am convinced that a man's most precious possession is a wise and loyal friend."
-**King Darius of Persia**.

"Loyalty to your comrades, when you come right down to it, has more to do with bravery in battle than even patriotism does. You may want to be brave, but your spirit can desert you when things really get rough. Only you find you can't let your comrades down and in the pinch they can't let you down either." -**Audie Murphy**

"Success is the result of perfection, hard work, learning from failure, loyalty, and persistence." -**General Colin Powell**

"For we are made for co-operation, like feet, like hands, like eyelids, like the rows of the upper and lower teeth. To act against one another, then, is contrary to nature; and it is acting against one another to be vexed and to turn away." -**Marcus Aurelius**

"So it is with the Spartans; fighting singly, they are as good as any, but fighting together, they are the best soldiers in the world." -**Demaratus**

"A band cemented by friendship…is never to be broken and thereby invincible." -**The historian Plutarch, describing the Sacred Band of Thebes, an elite squadron.**

"Thus what will gain the loyalty of officers are the forms of propriety. What will make the officers fight are the rewards. Treat them with the forms of propriety they like and reward them with what they love, then those you seek will come." -**Huang Shi Gong**

"Regard your soldiers as your children, and they will follow you into the deepest valleys; look upon them as your own beloved sons, and they will stand by you even unto death." -**Sun Tzu**

"But, after all, no man, however great his plastic skill, can hope to mould and shape a work of art to suit his fancy, unless the stuff on which he works be first prepared and made ready to obey the craftsman's will. Nor certainly where the raw material consists of men, will you succeed, unless, under God's blessing, these same men have been prepared and made ready to meet their officer in a friendly spirit. They must come to look upon him as of greater sagacity than themselves in all that concerns encounter with the enemy. This friendly disposition on the part of his subordinates, one must suppose, will best be fostered by a corresponding sympathy on the part of their commander towards the men themselves, and that not by simple kindness but by the obvious pains he takes on their behalf, at one time to provide them with food, and at another to secure safety of retreat, or again by help of outposts and the like, to ensure protection during rest and sleep."
**-Xenophon**

"The interval between the front and rear-rank men will best be filled supposing that the decadarchs (file leaders) are free to choose their own supports, and those chosen theirs, and so on following suit; since on this principle we may expect each man to have his trustiest comrade at his back." **-Xenophon**

"On the field of battle, it is a disgrace to the chief to be surpassed in valor by his companions, to the companions not to come up to the valor of their chiefs. As for leaving a battle alive after your chief has fallen, that means life-long infamy and shame. To defend and protect him, to put down one's own acts of heroism to his credit – that is what they mean by 'allegiance'. The chiefs fight for victory; the companions for their chiefs." **-The historian Tacitus, describing the Germanic warriors.**

"This I avow, that I will not flee a foot-space hence, but will press on and avenge my liege-lord in the fight… the steadfast heroes will have no need to reproach me not that may lord has fallen, that I made my way home and turned fro the battle, a lordless man. Rather shall weapon, spear-point and iron blade, be my end." **-Anonymous Saxon soldier recorded in *The Battle of Maldon.***

"Be not ashamed to be helped; for it is thy business to do thy duty like a soldier in the assault on a town. How then, if being lame thou canst not mount up on the battlements alone, but with the help of another, it is possible?" -**Marcus Aurelius**

"Together in danger, together in safety, [a good general's] army will be united together and never be split apart. The army can be employed but cannot be tired out. This is because of his beneficence, he ceaselessly gathers them together; with his plans he constantly unites them. Thus it is said that when you cultivate beneficence tirelessly. With one man, you can gain ten thousands more." -**Huang Shi Gong**

"I explained my idea of loyalty. When we are debating an issue, loyalty means giving me your honest opinion, whether you think I'll like it or not. Disagreement, at this stage, stimulates me. But once a decision has been made, the debate ends. From that point on, loyalty means executing the decision as if it were your own."-**General Colin Powell**

"I had the happiness to command a band of brothers." -**Horatio Nelson**

"If the officers despised the commanding general and have strong intent to return home... they can then be attacked and captured." -**Wu Qi**

"There, it all depends upon that article [a British infantry soldier] whether we do the business or not. Give me enough of it and I am sure."
-**Sir Arthur Wellesley, The Duke of Wellington**

"You have sworn loyalty to me. You have only one enemy, and that is my enemy."
-**Kaiser Wilhelm II**

"The officers and masses must be kept united." -**Huang Shi Gong**

"It is infinitely better to have a few good men than many indifferent ones."
**-George Washington**

"If a general shows confidence in his men but always insists on his orders being obeyed, the gain will be mutual." **-Sun Tzu**

"The file-leaders will depend upon the captain for the order passed along the line in what formation they are severally to march; and all being prearranged by word of mouth, the whole will work more smoothly than if left to chance—like people crowding out of a theatre to their mutual annoyance." **-Xenophon**

"Wherever the general's banner is, all the troops will go, and wherever the general points to, everyone will charge forward without concern for one's life." **-Wu Qi**

"We have come to a point where it is loyalty to resist, and treason to submit."
**-Carl Schurz**

"Loyalty to duty was shown by the Roman soldier of old who stuck to his post when the city of Pompeii was overwhelmed with ashes and lava from the volcano Vesuvius. His remains are still there, his hand covering his mouth and nose to prevent the suffocation which in the end overcame him." **-Robert Baden-Powell**

"But as his part *is* who goes down to the battle, so shall his part be who stays by the supplies; they shall share alike." **-King David**

"In general, of all principles of using troops, nothing surpasses unity. The unified can move like one entity and can depart like one entity." **-Jiang Taigong**

"Firstly you must always implicitly obey orders, without attempting to form any opinion of your own regarding their propriety. Secondly, you must consider every man your enemy who speaks ill of your king; and thirdly you must hate a Frenchman as you hate the devil." **-Horatio Nelson speaking to a midshipman aboard the Agamemnon (1793).**

"Now once the army have been brought together, they cannot be hastily separated." **-Huang Shi Gong**

"In the same way, a follower of the knights [i.e. one who follows their example] should be loyal to every one who is above him, whether his officers or his employers, and he should stick to them through thick and thin as part of his duty... He should be equally loyal to his family and friends, and should support them in evil times as well as in good times." **-Robert Baden-Powell**

"Control is achieved by training and management. At any time, discipline is strict; during war, they move and attack with awe. Their advancing and withdrawing stride is measured; the left and right look out for each other. Even if broken off from the main order, they preserve their formations; even if scattered they will reform lines. The whole army is very united and they share weal and woe together. When they are employed, they do not feel tired. No matter where you dispatch them, no one can withstand them." **-Wu Qi**

"We are very much like bricks in a wall; we each have our place, though it may seem a small one in so big a wall.  But if one brick crumbles or slips out of place, it begins to throw an undue strain on others, cracks appear and the wall totters." **-Robert Baden-Powell**

"People from the same village or districts should be grouped together, so that they can look out for each other." **-Wu Qi, on ordering the troops prior to battle.**

"Fight as bravely under me as you often have under the commander-in-chief; imagine that he is here, watching the battle in person." **-Julius Caesar, reporting the words of the commander Labienus.**

"Those who are naturally loyal say little about it, and are ready to assume it in others. In contrast, the type of soldier who is always dwelling on the importance of 'loyalty' usually means loyalty to his own interests." **-Captain Sir Basil Liddell Hart**

"When the generals are doubted, there will be mistrust. If the plans are doubted and not acted upon, the enemy will take the opportunity to attack." **-Huang Shi Gong**

"I only regret that I have but one life to lose for my country." **-Nathan Hale**

"When the men are punished before their loyalty is secured, they will be rebellious and disobedient. If disobedient and rebellious, it is difficult to deploy them. When the loyalty of the men is secured, but punishments are not enforced, such troops cannot be used either. Thus, the general must be able to instruct his troops with civility and humanity and unite them with rigorous training and discipline so as to secure victories in battles." **-Sun Tzu**

"We learn from history that those who are disloyal to their own superiors are most prone to preach loyalty to their subordinates. Loyalty is a noble quality, so long as it is not blind and does not exclude the higher loyalty to truth and decency. But the word is much abused. For 'loyalty,' analyzed, is too often a polite word for what would be more accurately described as 'a conspiracy for mutual inefficiency.' In this sense it is essentially selfish... 'loyalty' is not a quality we can isolate - so far as it is real, and of intrinsic value, it is implicit in the possession of other virtues." **-Captain Sir Basil Liddell Hart**

"The individual who refuses to defend his rights when called by his Government, deserves to be a slave, and must be punished as an enemy of his country and friend to her foe." -**Andrew Jackson**

"Loyalty is the big thing, the greatest battle asset of all. But no man ever wins the loyalty of troops by preaching loyalty. It is given him by them as he proves his possession of the other virtues. The doctrine of a blind loyalty to leadership is a selfish and futile military dogma except in so far as it is ennobled by a higher loyalty in all ranks to truth and decency." -**Brigadier-General S.L.A. Marshal**

"Those who would be military leaders must have loyal hearts, eyes and ears, claws and fangs. Without people loyal to them, they are like someone walking at night, not knowing where to step. Without eyes and ears, they are as though in the dark, not knowing where to proceed. Without claws and fangs, they are like hungry men eating poisoned food, inevitably they die... Therefore good generals always have intelligent and learned associates for their advisors, thoughtful and careful associates for their eyes and ears, brave and formidable associates for their claws and fangs." -**Zhuge Liang**

"It was a beautiful, calm, moonlight night. Suddenly a dog, which had been hiding under the clothes of a dead man, came up to us with a mournful howl, and then disappeared again immediately into his hiding place. He would lick his master's face, then run up to us again, only to return once more to his master. It seemed as if he were asking both for help and revenge. Whether it was the mood of the moment, whether it was the place, the time, the weather, or the action itself, or whatever it was, it is certainly true that nothing on any battlefield ever made such an impression on me. I involuntarily remained still, to observe the spectacle. This dead man, I said to myself, has perhaps friends, and he is lying here abandoned by all but his dog! What a lesson nature teaches us by means of an animal." -**Napoleon Bonaparte**

# Chapter 4
# Tactics and Strategy

*T*actics and strategies are where battles are lost and won, and tactics and strategies span a wide range of factors. Strategies are the larger-reaching plans: the decision to attack by sea rather than by land while making the enemy think that the attack will come by land. Tactics are also in the little details. These little details can range from mental and physical preparations and training to practical things like surveying the terrain to make it work in your favor, ensuring that supplies can get through and having the right equipment. Remember Robert Baden-Powell's advice that to be able to get a good night's sleep on bare ground can make the difference between defeat and victory (see Chapter 8 for a traditional English rhyme about small actions having big consequences).

---

"In battle like in siege, skill consists in converging a mass of fire on a single point: once the combat is opened, the commander who is adroit will suddenly and unexpectedly open fire with a surprising mass of artillery on one of these points, and is sure to seize it." -**Napoleon Bonaparte**

"Many men feel that they should act according to the time or the moment they are facing, and thus are in confusion when something goes beyond this and some difficulty arises." -**Shiba Yoshimasa**

"A man with deep far-sightedness will survey both the beginning and the end of a situation and continually consider its every facet as important." -**Takeda Shingen**

"In conflict, straightforward actions generally lead to engagement, surprising actions generally lead to victory." -**Sun Tzu**

"One arrow alone can be easily broken but many arrows are indestructible."
-**Genghis Khan**

"You will have to see, however, in retiring that your line of retreat is not right into the jaws of the enemy's reliefs hastening to the scene of action." -**Xenophon**

"The soft can counter the hard; the weak can counter the strong. Being soft at the appropriate extent can be a virtue; being inappropriately hard can be a menace."
-**Huang Shi Gong**

"Let nothing be done rashly, and at random, but all things according to the most exact and perfect rules of art." -**Marcus Aurelius**

"Strategy is the craft of the warrior. Commanders must enact the craft, and troopers should know this Way. There is no warrior in the world today who really understands the Way of strategy.... It is said the warrior's is the twofold Way of pen and sword, and he should have a taste for both Ways. Students of the Ichi School Way of strategy should train from the start with the sword and long sword in either hand. This is a truth: when you sacrifice your life, you must make fullest use of your weaponry. It is false not to do so, and to die with a weapon yet undrawn. In strategy, your spiritual bearing must not be any different from normal. Both in fighting and in everyday life, you should be determined though calm. Meet the situation without tenseness yet not recklessly, your spirit settled yet unbiased. If the enemy thinks of the mountains, attack like the sea; and if he thinks of the sea, attack like the mountains. If we watch men of other schools discussing theory, and concentrating on techniques with the hands, even though they seem skillful to watch, they have not the slightest true spirit." -**Miyamoto Musashi**

"The best way of avenging thyself is not to become like the wrong-doer."
**-Marcus Aurelius**

"Sacrifice the plum tree to preserve the peach tree." **-Thirty-Six Stratagems**

"The proper course, I say, is to appoint, with the concurrence of the several phylarchs [captains], certain decadarchs [file-leaders] to be selected from the men ripest of age and strength, most eager to achieve some deed of honour and to be known to fame. These are to form your front-rank men; and after these, a corresponding number should be chosen from the oldest and the most sagacious members of the squadron, to form the rear-rank of the files or decads; since, to use an illustration, iron best severs iron when the forefront of the blade is strong and tempered, and the momentum at the back is sufficient." **-Xenophon**

"Whatever may be snatched by ruse, thief fashion, your business is to send a competent patrol to seize." **-Xenophon**

"If you want to make peace, you don't talk to your friends. You talk to your enemies."
**-Moshe Dayan**

"Always run to the short way; and the short way is the natural: accordingly say and do everything in conformity with the soundest reason. For such a purpose frees a man from trouble, and warfare, and all artifice and ostentatious display." **-Marcus Aurelius**

"It would be no bad thing either, to forewarn your troopers that one day you will take them out yourself for a long march, and lead them across country over every kind of ground." **-Xenophon**

"If they [the enemy] are found to be in chaos, do not hesitate to attack them." **-Wu Qi**

"To ... not prepare is the greatest of crimes; to be prepared beforehand for any contingency is the greatest of virtues." -**Sun Tzu**

"There is but one means to extenuate the effects of enemy fire: it is to develop a more violent fire oneself." -**Ferdinand Foch**

"We must make this campaign an exceedingly active one. Only thus can a weaker country cope with a stronger; it must make up in activity what it lacks in strength. A defensive campaign can only be made successful by taking the aggressive at the proper time. Napoleon never waited for his adversary to become fully prepared, but struck him the first blow." -**Stonewall Jackson**

"An army too numerous is subject to many dangers and inconveniences. Its bulk makes it slow and unwieldy in its motions; and as it is obliged to march in columns of great length, it is exposed to the risk of being continually harassed and insulted by inconsiderable parties of the enemy. The incumbrance of the baggage is often an occasion of its being surprised in its passage through difficult places or over rivers. The difficulty of providing forage for such numbers of horses and other beasts of burden is very great. Besides, scarcity of provisions, which is to be carefully guarded against in all expeditions, soon ruins such large armies where the consumption is so prodigious, that notwithstanding the greatest care in filling the magazines they must begin to fail in a short time. And sometimes they unavoidably will be distressed for want of water. But, if unfortunately this immense army should be defeated, the numbers lost must necessarily be very great, and the remainder, who save themselves by flight, too much dispirited to be brought again to action. The ancients, taught by experience, preferred discipline to numbers." -**Publius Flavius Vegetius Renatus**

"Kill with a borrowed knife." -**Thirty-Six Stratagems**

"Rapidity is the essence of war: take advantage of the enemy's unreadiness, make your way by unexpected routes, and attack unguarded spots." -**Sun Tzu**

"Confine thyself to the present. Understand well what happens either to thee or to another." -**Marcus Aurelius**

"Soft, hard, weak and strong: each has its appropriate place, and one should combining these four and use them where it is most appropriate." -**Huang Shi Gong**

"I have a high art: I hurt with cruelty those who would damage me." -**Archilochus**

"I wish to have no connection with any ship that does not sail fast; for I intend to go in harm's way." -**Admiral John Paul Jones**

"Make a sound in the east, then strike in the west." -**Thirty-Six Stratagems**

"So, too, with regard to spies and intelligencers. Before war commences your business is to provide yourself with a supply of people friendly to both states, or maybe merchants (since states are ready to receive the importer of goods with open arms); sham deserters may be found occasionally useful. Not, of course, that the confidence you feel in your spies must ever cause you to neglect outpost duty; indeed your state of preparation should at any moment be precisely what it ought to be, supposing the approach or the imminent arrival of the enemy were to be announced. Let a spy be ever so faithful, there is always the risk he may fail to report his intelligence at the critical moment, since the obstacles which present themselves in war are not to be counted on the fingers."
-**Xenophon**

"Adapt thyself to the things with which thy lot has been cast." -**Marcus Aurelius**

"One who makes preparation after the battle has been lost is not a superior sage. One whose skill is the same as the masses is not a superior artisan." -**Jiang Taigong**

"You must concentrate upon and consecrate yourself wholly to each day, as though a fire were raging in your hair." -**Taisen Deshimaru**

"Battles are won by frightening the enemy. Fear is induced by inflicting death and wounds on him. Death and wounds are produced by fire. Fire from the rear is more deadly and three times more effective than fire from the front, but to get fire behind the enemy, you must hold him by frontal fire and move rapidly around his flank."
-**General Patton**

"There is still a tendency in each separate unit... to be a one-handed puncher. By that I mean that the rifleman wants to shoot, the tanker to charge, the artillery-man to fire... That is not the way to win battles. If the band played a piece first with the piccolo, then with the brass horn, then with the clarinet, and then with the trumpet, there would be a hell of a lot of noise but no music. To get the harmony in music each instrument must support the others. To get harmony in battle, each weapon must support the other. Team play wins. You musicians of Mars must not wait for the band leader to signal you... You must each of your own volition see to it that you come into this concert at the proper place and at the proper time." -**General Patton**

"The technique for military conquest is to carefully investigate the enemy's intentions and quickly take advantage of them, launching a sudden attack where unexpected."
-**Jiang Taigong**

"The best safeguard against failure in any attempt to enforce pursuit or conduct a retreat lies in a thorough knowledge of your horse's powers. But how is this experience to be got? Simply by paying attention to their behaviour in the peaceable manouvres of the sham fight, when there is no real enemy to intervene--how the animals come off, in fact, and what stamina they show in the various charges and retreats." -**Xenophon**

"Or take the case: the enemy is on the march in some direction, and a portion of his force becomes detached from his main body or through excess of confidence is caught straggling; do not let the opportunity escape, but make it a rule always to pursue a weaker with a stronger force. These, indeed, are rules of procedure, which it only requires a simple effort of the mind to appreciate. Creatures far duller of wit than man have this ability: kites and falcons, when anything is left unguarded, pounce and carry it off and retire into safety without being caught; or wolves, again, will hunt down any quarry left widowed of its guard, or thieve what they can in darksome corners. In case a dog pursues and overtakes them, should he chance to be weaker the wolf attacks him, or if stronger, the wolf will slaughter his quarry and make off. At other times, if the pack be strong enough to make light of the guardians of a flock, they will marshal their battalions, as it were, some to drive off the guard and others to effect the capture, and so by stealth or fair fight they provide themselves with the necessaries of life. I say, if dumb beasts are capable of conducting a raid with so much sense and skill, it is hard if any average man cannot prove himself equally intelligent with creatures which themselves fall victims to the craft of man." **-Xenophon**


"Attack the strong through growing his arrogance." **-Jiang Taigong**


"Wipe out imagination: check desire: extinguish appetite: keep the ruling faculty in its own power." **-Marcus Aurelius**


"To know in war how to recognize an opportunity and seize it is better than anything else." **-Machiavelli**


"Let the body itself take care, if it can, that it suffer nothing, and let it speak, if it suffers." **-Marcus Aurelius**


"Create something from nothing." **-Thirty-Six Stratagems**

"The enemy is less likely to get wind of an advance of cavalry, if the orders for march were passed from mouth to mouth rather than announced by voice of herald, or public notice." -**Xenophon**

"Everyone covets strength and power, but rare are those who are capable of using softness and weakness appropriately." -**Huang Shi Gong**

"What is of the greatest importance in war is extraordinary speed: One cannot afford to neglect opportunity." -**Sun Tzu**

"The art of war is, in the last result, the art of keeping one's freedom of action." -**Xenophon**

"Everywhere and at all times it is in thy power piously to acquiesce in thy present condition, and to behave justly to those who are about thee, and to exert thy skill upon thy present thoughts, that nothing shall steal into them without being well examined." -**Marcus Aurelius**

"The art of life is more like the wrestler's art than the dancer's, in respect of this, that it should stand ready and firm to meet onsets which are sudden and unexpected." -**Marcus Aurelius**

"When an advanced guard is needed, I say for myself I highly approve of secret pickets and outposts, if only because in supplying a guard to protect your friends you are contriving an ambuscade to catch the enemy. Also the outposts will be less exposed to a secret attack, being themselves unseen, and yet a source of great alarm to the enemy; since the bare knowledge that there are outposts somewhere, though where precisely no man knows, will prevent the enemy from feeling confident, and oblige him to mistrust every tenable position. An exposed outpost, on the contrary, presents to the broad eye of day its dangers and also its weaknesses." -**Xenophon**

"It is easy to kill someone with a slash of a sword. It is hard to be impossible for others to cut down." -**Yagyu Munenori**

"In tactics every engagement, great or small, is a defensive one if we leave the initiative to the enemy." -**Karl von Clausewitz**

"In a major campaign, everyone should be trained to use the equipment."
-**Jiang Taigong**

"To be prepared for war is one of the most effective means of preserving peace."
-**George Washington, quoting the Roman military tactician Publius Flavius Vegetius Renatus.**

"It is much better to tempt fortune where it can favor you than to see your certain ruin by not tempting it." -**Machiavelli**

"Everything can collapse. Houses, bodies, and enemies collapse when their rhythm becomes deranged. In large-scale strategy, when the enemy starts to collapse you must pursue him without letting the chance go. If you fail to take advantage of your enemies' collapse, they may recover." -**Miyamoto Musashi**

"There is timing in everything. Timing in strategy cannot be mastered without a great deal of practice." -**Miyamoto Musashi**

"'To become the enemy' means to think yourself into the enemy's position. In the world people tend to think of a robber trapped in a house as a fortified enemy. However, if we think of 'becoming the enemy', we feel that the whole world is against us and that there is no escape. He who is shut inside is a pheasant. He who enters to arrest is a hawk. You must appreciate this." -**Miyamoto Musashi**

"Disintegration happens to everything. When a house crumbles, a person crumbles, or an adversary crumbles, they fall apart by getting out of rhythm with the times.

In the art of war on a large scale, it is also essential to find the rhythm of opponents as they come apart, and pur-sue them so as not to let openings slip by. If you miss the timing of vulnerable moments, there is the likelihood of counterattack.

In the individual art of war it also happens that an adversary will get out of rhythm in combat and start to fall apart. If you let such a chance get by you, the adversary will recover and thwart you. It is essential to follow up firmly on any loss of poise on the part of an adversary, to prevent the opponent from recovering." -**Miyamoto Musashi**

"See the possibilities and advance, know the difficulties and withdraw." -**Wu Qi**

"In order to capture, one must let loose." -**Thirty-Six Stratagems**

"Thus it is said that if one fights before understanding the situation, even if he is more numerous, he will certainly be defeated." -**Jiang Taigong**

"In the first place, let it be a fundamental rule, if possible, not to attempt to delude the enemy at close quarters; distance, as it aids illusion, will promote security." -**Xenophon**

"It is the business rather of the cavalry general to recognise at a glance the sort of ground on which infantry will be superior to cavalry and where cavalry will be superior to infantry. He should be a man of invention, ready of device to turn all circumstances to account, so as to give at one time a small body of cavalry the appearance of a larger, and again a large the likeness of a smaller body; he should have the craft to appear absent when close at hand, and within striking distance when a long way off; he should know exactly not only how to steal an enemy's position, but by a master stroke of cunning to spirit his own cavalry away, and, when least expected, deliver his attack." -**Xenophon**

"If you do not look at things on a large scale it will be difficult for you to master strategy." -**Miyamoto Musashi**

"The general, before he puts his troops in motion, should send out detachments of trusty and experienced soldiers well mounted, to reconnoiter the places through which he is to march, in front, in rear, and on the right and left, lest he should fall into ambuscades. The night is safer and more advantageous for your spies to do their business in than day, for if they are taken prisoners, you have, as it were, betrayed yourself. After this, the cavalry should march off first, then the infantry; the baggage, bat horses, servants and carriages follow in the center; and part of the best cavalry and infantry come in the rear, since it is oftener attacked on a march than the front. The flanks of the baggage, exposed to frequent ambuscades, must also be covered with a sufficient guard to secure them. But above all, the part where the enemy is most expected must be reinforced with some of the best cavalry, light infantry and foot archers." -**Publius Flavius Vegetius Renatus**

"Labor not as one who is wretched, nor yet as one who would be pitied or admired."
-**Marcus Aurelius**

"Being as swift as the flying arrow and attacking as suddenly as the release of a crossbow are the ways by which to destroy brilliant plans." -**Jiang Taigong**

"Tossing out a brick to get a jade gem." -**Thirty-Six Stratagems**

"Whoever can surprise well must conquer." -**Admiral John Paul Jones**

"The good fighters of old first put themselves beyond the possibility of defeat, and then waited for an opportunity of defeating the enemy." -**Sun Tzu**

"Defeat the enemy by capturing their chief." -**Thirty-Six Stratagems**

"When you are in any contest you should work as if there were – to the very last minute – a chance to lose it." -**Dwight D. Eisenhower**

"Thus we may know that there are five essentials for victory:

(1) He will win who knows when to fight and when not to fight.

(2) He will win who knows how to handle both superior and inferior forces.

(3) He will win whose army is animated by the same spirit throughout all its ranks.

(4) He will win who, prepared himself, waits to take the enemy unprepared.

(5) He will win who has military capacity and is not interfered with by the sovereign."
-**Sun Tzu**

"A cavalry commander should also devise tricks of his own, suitable for his situation. The basic point is that deceit is your most valuable asset in war... If you think about it, you will find that the majority of important military successes have come about as a result of trickery. It follows, then, that if you are to take on the office of commander, you should ask the gods to allow you to count the ability to deceive among your qualifications, and should also work on it yourself." -**Xenophon**

"When the equipment to be used by the army is fully prepared, what worries will the commander-in-chief have?" -**Jiang Taigong**

"There is nothing as likely to succeed as what the enemy believes you cannot attempt."
-**Machiavelli**

"If the enemy approaches in large numbers but in disarray, their flags and formations are in a mess and the troops frequently look about, by using one tenth of their strength, we can invariably cause them to be helpless." -**Wu Qi**

"When a thing is done, it's done. Don't look back. Look forward to your next objective."
**-George C. Marshall**


"The body ought to be compact, and to show no irregularity either in motion or attitude. For what the mind shows in the face by maintaining in it the expression of intelligence and propriety, that ought to be required also in the whole body. But all these things should be observed without affectation." **-Marcus Aurelius**


"If the problem be to make large numbers appear small, supposing you have ground at command adapted to concealment, the thing is simple: by leaving a portion of your men exposed and hiding away a portion in obscurity, you may effect your object."
**-Xenophon**


"The method that the men use for leveling the fields is the same for attacking walls. The skill needed in spring to cut down grass and thickets is the same as needed for fighting against chariots and cavalry. The weeding method used in summer is the same as used in battle against foot soldiers." **-Jiang Taigong**


"A battle is commonly decided in two or three hours, after which no further hopes are left for the worsted army. Every plan, therefore, is to be considered, every expedient tried and every method taken before matters are brought to this last extremity. Good officers decline general engagements where the danger is common, and prefer the employment of stratagem and finesse to destroy the enemy as much as possible in detail and intimidate them without exposing our own forces."
**-Publius Flavius Vegetius Renatus**


"Seek opportunity to trick the enemy and quickly get away, setting up ambushes to your rear." **-Jiang Taigong**

"Those who have courage and strength should be assembled into a unit. Those who take pleasure in advancing into battle and exerting their strength so as to manifest their loyalty and courage should be assembled into another unit. Those who are nimble and fleet should be assembled into another unit. Officials who have lost their position and are eager to make amends should be assembled into a unit. Those who have lost in war and want to eradicate their disgrace should be assembled into a unit. These five will serve to be the elite troops. With three thousands of such men, one can then break any encirclement or break into any cities." -**Wu Qi**

"Feign madness but keep your balance." -**Thirty-Six Stratagems**

"In large-scale strategy, it is beneficial to strike at the corners of the enemy's force, If the corners are overthrown, the spirit of the whole body will be overthrown."
-**Miyamoto Musashi**

"When the enemy moves observe him; when he approaches, prepare for him."
-**Huang Shi Gong**

"When the enemy is close at hand and remains quiet, he is relying on the natural strength of his position. When he keeps aloof and tries to provoke a battle, he is anxious for the other side to advance. If his place of encampment is easy of access, he is tendering a bait." -**Sun Tzu**

"When you attain the Way of strategy there will not be one thing you cannot see. You must study hard." -**Miyamoto Musashi**

"The art of war is simple enough. Find out where your enemy is. Get at him as soon as you can. Strike him as hard as you can, and keep moving on." -**Ulysses S. Grant**

"In every battle there comes a time when both sides consider themselves beaten, then he who continues the attack wins." -**Ulysses S. Grant**

"You may work on the enemy's fears by the various devices of mock ambuscades, sham relief parties, false information. Conversely, his confidence will reach an overweening pitch, if the idea gets abroad that his opponents have troubles of their own and little leisure for offensive operations." -**Xenophon**

"The greatest remedy that is used against a plan of the enemy is to do voluntarily what he plans that you do by force." -**Machiavelli**

"Those who are skilful in employing their forces will manage a victory. Those who are not will perish." -**Jiang Taigong**

"Set our pennants and flags out on high and carefully maneuver the army without letting the enemy know our true situation." -**Jiang Taigong**

"War is essentially a calculation of probabilities." -**Napoleon Bonaparte**

"Remove the ladder when the enemy has ascended to the roof."
-**Thirty-Six Stratagems**

"When the enemy is relaxed, make them toil. When full, starve them. When settled, make them move." -**Sun Tzu**

"Look within. Within is the fountain of good, and it will ever bubble up, if thou wilt ever dig." -**Marcus Aurelius**

"The situations you can attack an enemy:

1. When the enemy has just arrived from afar and their battle formations are not yet properly formed and deployed, they can be attacked.

2. If they have just eaten and not yet established their encampment, they can be attacked.

3. If they are on the move and the troops formation is disarray, they can be attacked.

4. If they have labored hard, they can be attacked.

5. If they have not seized the advantages of the terrain, they can be attacked.

6. When they have not seized the critical timing, they can be attacked.

7. When their flags and banners move about chaotically, they can be attacked.

8. When they have traversed a great distance, their supplies and reinforcement just arrived and the whole troops have not rested, they can be attacked.

9. When crossing the river and only half of them have crossed, they can be attacked.

10. On treacherous terrain or narrow roads, they can be attacked.

11. The formations changes frequently, they can be attacked.

12. When a general is separated from his soldiers, they can be attacked.

13. When they are afraid, they can be attacked." -**Wu Qi**


"If the enemy is strong and his morale is high, be deferential in order to make him more arrogant." -**Huang Shi Gong**


"If the enemy approaches, when they see our state of readiness and alertness, they will certainly turn around. As a result, their strength will become exhausted and their spirits dejected." -**Jiang Taigong**

"The ability of a commander to comprehend a situation and act promptly is the talent which great men have of conceiving in a moment all the advant-ages of the terrain and the use that they can make of it with their army. When you are accustomed to the size of your army you soon form your coup d'oeil with reference to it, and habit teaches you the ground that you can occupy with a certain number of troops.

Use of this talent is of great importance on two occasions. First, when you encounter the enemy on your march and are obliged instantly to choose ground on which to fight. As I have remarked, within a single square mile a hundred different orders of battle can be formed. The clever general perceives the advantages of the terrain instantly; he gains advantage from the slightest hillock, from a tiny marsh; he advances or withdraws a wing to gain superiority; he strengthens either his right or his left, moves ahead or to the rear, and profits from the merest bagatelles." -**Frederick the Great**


"The reasonable course of action in any use of arms starts with calculation. Before fighting, first assess the relative sagacity of the military leadership, the relative strength of the enemy, the size of the armies, the lay of the land, and the adequacy of provisions. If you send troops out only after making these calculations, you will never fail to win." -**Liu Ji**


"The essence of the principles of warriors is responding to changes; expertise is a matter of knowing the military. In any action it is imperative to assess the enemy first. If opponents show no change or movement, then wait for them. Take advantage of change to respond accordingly, and you will benefit.

The rule is 'The ability to gain victory by changing and adapting according to opponents is called genius.'" -**Liu Ji**


"In general, being alert to danger is the true measure of good governance, ensuring the security of the state. As you have now recognized, the importance of being cautious, disaster can be kept away." -**Wu Qi**

"Wherever the enemy goes, let our troops go also." -**Ulysses S. Grant**

"Do not fret – it only causes harm." -**King David**

"Troops must never be engaged in a general action immediately after a long march, when the men are fatigued and the horses tired. The strength required for action is spent in the toil of the march. What can a soldier do who charges when out of breath?" -**Publius Flavius Vegetius Renatus**

"Everyone has his superstitions. One of mine has always been when I started to go anywhere, or to do anything, never to turn back or to stop until the thing intended was accomplished." -**Ulysses S. Grant**

"Inflict injury on oneself to win the enemy's trust." -**Thirty-Six Stratagems**

"Simulated disorder postulates perfect discipline, simulated fear postulates courage; simulated weakness postulates strength." -**Sun Tzu**

"If you occupy the left side of a mountain, you must urgently prepare against an attack from the right side. If you occupy the right side of a mountain, then you should urgently prepare against an attack from the left." -**Jiang Taigong**

"'Safety first' is the road to ruin in war." -**Winston Churchill**

"You must never believe that the enemy does not know how to conduct his own affairs. Indeed, if you want to be deceived less and want to bear less danger, the more the enemy is weak or the less the enemy is cautious, so much more must you esteem him." -**Machiavelli**

"This is as true in everyday life as it is in battle: we are given one life and the decision is ours whether to wait for circumstances to make up our mind, or whether to act, and in acting, to live." -**Omar Bradley**

"But there will be a great rise in their spirits if one can change the way they think, so that instead of having in their heads the one idea of 'what is going to happen to me?' they may think 'what action am I going to take?" -**Xenophon**

"If we have to fight a battle, what we must see to is how we may fight with the greatest efficiency." -**Xenophon**.

"No one has ever died in battle through being bitten or kicked by a horse; it is men who do whatever gets done in battle." -**Xenophon**

"The art of war, then, is governed by five constant factors, to be taken into account in one's deliberations, when seeking to determine the conditions obtaining in the field. These are: (1) The Moral Law; (2) Heaven; (3) Earth; (4) The Commander; (5) Method and discipline. The Moral Law causes the people to be in complete accord with their ruler, so that they will follow him regardless of their lives, undismayed by any danger. Heaven signifies night and day, cold and heat, times and seasons. Earth comprises distances, great and small; danger and security; open ground and narrow passes; the chances of life and death. The Commander stands for the virtues of wisdom, sincerely, benevolence, courage and strictness. By method and discipline are to be understood the marshalling of the army in its proper subdivisions, the graduations of rank among the officers, the maintenance of roads by which supplies may reach the army, and the control of military expenditure. These five heads should be familiar to every general: he who knows them will be victorious; he who knows them not will fail." -**Sun Tzu**

"Let us get rid of all inessentials in the rest of our equipment." -**Xenophon**

"If everything else fails, retreat." -**Thirty-Six Stratagems**


"In drawing up an army in order of battle, three things are to be considered: the sun, the dust and the wind...Our troops should be so disposed as to have these inconveniences behind them, while they are directly in the enemy's front."
-**Publius Flavius Vegetius Renatus**


"According as circumstances are favorable, one should modify one's plans." -**Sun Tzu**


"When about to engage in combat, determine the wind direction. If upwind, yell and charge in the direction of the wind, if contrary, maintain formation and wait for opportunity to attack." -**Wu Qi**


"Once war is forced upon us, there is no alternative than to apply every available means to bring it to a swift end. War's very object is victory – not prolonged indecision."
-**Douglas MacArthur**


"There is no security on this earth; there is only opportunity." -**Douglas MacArthur**


"The war shout should not be begun till both armies have joined, for it is a mark of ignorance or cowardice to give it at a distance. The effect is much greater on the enemy when they find themselves struck at the same instant with the horror of the noise and the points of the weapons." -**Publius Flavius Vegetius Renatus**


"The best luck of all is the luck you make for yourself." -**Douglas MacArthur**


"It is fatal to enter any war without the will to win it." -**Douglas MacArthur**

"In war there is no substitute for victory." **-Douglas MacArthur**

"An able general never loses a favorable opportunity of surprising the enemy either when tired on the march, divided in the passage of a river, embarrassed in morasses, struggling with the declivities of mountains, when dispersed over the country they think themselves in security or are sleeping in their quarters."
**-Publius Flavius Vegetius Renatus**

"The clever combatant imposes his will on the enemy, but does not allow the enemy's will to be imposed on him." **-Sun Tzu**

"Knowledge dominance does scare us as Marines. General George Armstrong Custer probably thought he had knowledge dominance, too. Any time you think you're smarter than your adversary, you're probably about a half-mile from the Little Big Horn."
**-Colonel Art Corbett**

"It is far more important to be able to hit the target than it is to haggle over who makes a weapon or who pulls a trigger." **-Dwight D. Eisenhower**

"I will either find a way, or make one." **-Hannibal**

"The more your troops have been accustomed to camp duties on frontier stations and the more carefully they have been disciplined, the less danger they will be exposed to in the field." **-Publius Flavius Vegetius Renatus**

"Because a thing seems difficult for you, do not think it impossible for anyone to accomplish." **-Marcus Aurelius**

"However military skill is no less necessary in general actions than in carrying on war by subtlety and stratagem." -**Publius Flavius Vegetius Renatus**

"Appear at points which the enemy must hasten to defend; march swiftly to places where you are not expected." -**Sun Tzu**

"You don't hurt 'em if you don't hit 'em." -**Lewis Burwell "Chesty" Puller**

"Being ready is not what matters. What matters is winning after you get there." -**Lieutenant General Victor H. Krulak, USMC**

"Sometimes it is entirely appropriate to kill a fly with a sledge-hammer!" -**Maj. Holdredge**

"Remember upon the conduct of each depends the fate of all." -**Alexander the Great**

"There is nothing impossible to him who will try." -**Alexander the Great**

"The art of war does not require complicated maneuvers; the simplest are the best, and common sense is fundamental. From which one might wonder how it is generals make blunders; it is because they try to be clever. The most difficult thing is to guess the enemy's plan, to sift the truth from all the reports that come in. The rest merely requires common sense; it is like a boxing match, the more you punch the better it is. It is also necessary to read the map well." -**Napoleon Bonaparte**

"Never interrupt your enemy when he is making a mistake." -**Napoleon Bonaparte**

"If you want a thing done well, do it yourself." -**Napoleon Bonaparte**

"The battlefield is a scene of constant chaos. The winner will be the one who controls that chaos, both his own and the enemies." -**Napoleon Bonaparte**

"Military science consists in calculating all the chances accurately in the first place, and then in giving accident exactly, almost mathematically, its place in one's calculations. It is upon this point that one must not deceive oneself, and yet a decimal more or less may change all. Now this apportioning of accident and science cannot get into any head except that of a genius... Accident, hazard, chance, call it what you may, a mystery to ordinary minds, becomes a reality to superior men." -**Napoleon Bonaparte**

"Take time to deliberate, but when the time for action has arrived, stop thinking and go in." -**Napoleon Bonaparte**

"One should never forbid what one lacks the power to prevent." -**Napoleon Bonaparte**

"One must change one's tactics every ten years if one wishes to maintain one's superiority." -**Napoleon Bonaparte**

"Nothing is more difficult, and therefore more precious, than to be able to decide."
-**Napoleon Bonaparte**

"In war, there is but one favorable moment; the great art is to seize it!"
-**Napoleon Bonaparte**

"In order to govern, the question is not to follow out a more or less valid theory but to build with whatever materials are at hand. The inevitable must be accepted and turned to advantage." -**Napoleon Bonaparte**

"The issue of a battle is the result of a single instant, a single thought. The adversaries come into each other's presence with various combinations; they mingle; they fight for a length of time; the decisive moment appears; a psychological spark makes the decision; and a few reserved troops are enough to carry it out." -**Napoleon Bonaparte**

"You must not fight too often with one enemy, or you will teach him all your art of war." -**Napoleon Bonaparte**

"A good plan executed today is better than a perfect plan executed at some indefinite point in the future." -**General Patton**

"Take calculated risks. This is quite different from being rash." -**General Patton**

"Wars may be fought with weapons, but they are won by men." -**General Patton**

"Infantry must move forward to close with the enemy. It must shoot in order to move… To halt under fire is folly. To halt under fire and not fire back is suicide. Officers must set the example." -**General Patton**

"War is an art and as such is not susceptible of explanation by fixed formula."
-**General Patton**

"Invincibility lies in the defense; the possibility of victory in the attack." -**Sun Tzu**

"Now the general who wins a battle makes many calculations in his temple ere the battle is fought. The general who loses a battle makes but few calculations beforehand. Thus do many calculations lead to victory, and few calculations to defeat: How much more no calculation at all! It is by attention to this point that I can see who is likely to win."
-**Sun Tzu**

"Those who are first on the battlefield and await the opponents are at ease; those who are last on the battlefield and head into a fight become exhausted. Therefore, good warriors cause others to go to them and do not go to others." -**Sun Tzu**

"All warfare is based on deception. Hence, when able to attack, we must seem unable; when using our forces we must seem inactive; when we are near, we must make the enemy believe that we are away; when far away, we must make him believe we are near. Hold out baits to entice the enemy. Feign disorder, and crush him. If he is secure at all points, be prepared for him. If he is in superior strength, evade him. If your opponent is of choleric temper, seek to irritate him. Pretend to be weak, that he may grow arrogant. If he is taking his ease, give him no rest. If his forces are united, separate them. Attack him where he is unprepared, appear where you are not expected." -**Sun Tzu**

"To fight and conquer in all our battles is not supreme excellence; supreme excellence consists in breaking the enemy's resistance without fighting." -**Sun Tzu**

"Victorious warriors win first and then go to war, while defeated warriors go to war first and then seek to win." -**Sun Tzu**

"He who knows when he can fight and when he cannot, will be victorious." -**Sun Tzu**

"Thus, what is of supreme importance in war is to attack the enemy's strategy."
-**Sun Tzu**

"The dance of battle is always played to the same impatient rhythm. What begins in a surge of violent motion is always reduced to the perfectly still." -**Sun Tzu**

"Pretend inferiority and encourage his arrogance." -**Sun Tzu**

"The good fighters of old first put themselves beyond the possibility of defeat, and then waited for an opportunity of defeating the enemy." -**Sun Tzu**

"Strategy without tactics is the slowest route to victory. Tactics without strategy is the noise before defeat." -**Sun Tzu**

"Now the reason the enlightened prince and the wise general conquer the enemy whenever they move and their achievements surpass those of ordinary men is foreknowledge." -**Sun Tzu**

"If you are far from the enemy, make him believe you are near." -**Sun Tzu**

"If ignorant both of your enemy and yourself, you are certain to be in peril." -**Sun Tzu**

"For to win one hundred victories in one hundred battles is not the acme of skill. To subdue the enemy without fighting is the acme of skill." -**Sun Tzu**

"All men can see these tactics whereby I conquer, but what none can see is the strategy out of which victory is evolved." -**Sun Tzu**

"Victory is reserved for those who are willing to pay its price." -**Sun Tzu**

"See first with your mind, then with your eyes, and finally with your body."
-**Yagyu Munenori**

"When the swords flash, let no idea of love, piety, or even the face of your fathers move you." -**Julius Caesar**

"The more you sweat in training, the less you will bleed in battle."
**-Motto of Navy Seals**


"Given the same amount of intelligence, timidity will do a thousand times more damage than audacity." **-Karl von Clausewitz**


"There is only one decisive victory: the last." **-Karl von Clausewitz**


"The majority of people are timid by nature, and that is why they constantly exaggerate danger. All influences on the military leader, therefore, combine to give him a false impression of his opponent's strength, and from this arises a new source of indecision."
**-Karl von Clausewitz**


"The best form of defense is attack." **-Karl von Clausewitz**


"No one starts a war-or rather, no one in his senses ought to do so-without first being clear in his mind what he intends to achieve by that war and how he intends to conduct it." **-Karl von Clausewitz**


"Pursue one great decisive aim with force and determination." **-Karl von Clausewitz**


"If the enemy is to be coerced, you must put him in a situation that is even more unpleasant than the sacrifice you call on him to make. The hardships of the situation must not be merely transient - at least not in appearance. Otherwise, the enemy would not give in, but would wait for things to improve." **-Karl von Clausewitz**


"A dream doesn't become reality through magic; it takes sweat, determination and hard work." **-General Colin Powell**

"The first and most important rule to observe...is to use our entire forces with the utmost energy. The second rule is to concentrate our power as much as possible against that section where the chief blows are to be delivered and to incur disadvantages elsewhere, so that our chances of success may increase at the decisive point. The third rule is never to waste time. Unless important advantages are to be gained from hesitation, it is necessary to set to work at once. By this speed a hundred enemy measures are nipped in the bud, and public opinion is won most rapidly. Finally, the fourth rule is to follow up our successes with the utmost energy. Only pursuit of the beaten enemy gives the fruits of victory." -**Karl von Clausewitz**

"Only great and general battles can produce great results." -**Karl von Clausewitz**

"A state can indulge in armed invasion only where, by invasion, it can reduce the power of an enemy without in any way reducing its own potential, by making suitable arrangements for protection of its own strategic works." -**Kautilya**

"Military tactics are like unto water; for water in its natural course runs away from high places and hastens downwards. So in war, the way is to avoid what is strong and to strike at what is weak.

Water shapes its course according to the nature of the ground over which it flows; the soldier works out his victory in relation to the foe whom he is facing. Therefore, just as water retains no constant shape, so in warfare there are no constant conditions.
He who can modify his tactics in relation to his opponent and thereby succeed in winning, may be called a heaven-born captain." -**Sun Tzu**

"Perpetual optimism is a force multiplier." -**General Colin Powell**

"We may take it then that an army without its baggage-train is lost; without provisions it is lost; without bases of supply it is lost." -**Sun Tzu**

"In a man-to-man fight, the winner is he who has one more round in his magazine."
**-Erwin Rommel**


"Every soldier must know, before he goes into battle, how the little battle he is to fight fits into the larger picture, and how the success of his fighting will influence the battle as a whole." **-Bernard Law Montgomery**


"Let your rapidity be that of the wind, your compactness that of the forest. In raiding and plundering be like fire; in immovability like a mountain. Let your plans be dark and impenetrable as night, and when you move, fall like a thunderbolt." **-Sun Tzu**


"The best troops of the State are the regulars." **-Frederick the Great**


"Entering into a treaty is peace. Doing injury is war. Remaining indifferent is staying quiet. Augmenting power is marching. Submitting to another is seeking shelter. Resorting to peace with one and war with another is dual policy. These are the six measures of foreign policy." **-Kautilya**


"It is much easier to march uphill without fighting than to march on the level when one has enemies on all sides; and one can see what is in front of one's feet better by night when one is not fighting, than by day if one is; and rough ground is easier for the feet, if one is not fighting as one marches, than level ground is, when there are weapons flying round one's head." **-Xenophon**


"A good plan violently executed right now is far better than a perfect plan executed next week." **-General George Patton**


"In war: resolution. In defeat: defiance. In victory: magnanimity. In peace: goodwill."
**-Winston Churchill**

"Don't fight a battle if you don't gain anything by winning." -**Erwin Rommel**

"My home policy: I wage war; my foreign policy: I wage war. All the time, I wage war." -**Georges Clemenceau**

"In preparing for battle, I have always found that plans are useless, but planning is indispensable." -**Dwight D. Eisenhower**

"No proceeding is better than that which you have concealed from the enemy until the time you have executed it. To know how to recognize an opportunity in war, and take it, benefits you more than anything else. Nature creates few men brave; industry and training makes many. Discipline in war counts more than fury." -**Machiavelli**

"Battle should no longer resemble a bludgeon fight, but should be a test of skill, a manoeuvre combat, in which is fulfilled the great principle of surprise by striking 'from an unexpected direction against an unguarded spot.'" -**Captain Sir Basil Liddell Hart**

"But the complete Roman legion, in its own peculiar cohorts, contains within itself the heavy-armed foot...the lightarmed foot... together with the legionary cavalry incorporated with it. These bodies, all actuated with the same spirit, are united inseparably in their various dispositions for forming, encamping and fighting. Thus the legion is compact and perfect in all its parts and, without any foreign assistance, has always been superior to any force that could be brought against it. The Roman greatness is a proof of the excellence of their legions, for with them they always defeated whatever numbers of the enemy they thought fit, or their circumstances gave them an opportunity to engage." -**Publius Flavius Vegetius Renatus**

"Philosophers and scientists have shown that adaptation is the secret of existence. History, however, is a catalogue of failures to change in time with the need. And armies, which because of their role should be the most adaptable of institutions, have been the most rigid - to the cost of the causes they upheld. Almost every great soldier of the past has borne witness to this truth. But it needs no such personal testimony, for the facts of history, unhappily, prove it in overwhelming array. No one can in honesty ignore them if he has once examined them. And to refrain from emphasizing them would be a crime against the country. For it amounts to complicity after the event, which is even more culpable when the life of a people, not merely of one person, is concerned. In the latter case there may be some excuse for discreet silence, as your testimony cannot restore the dead person to life. But in the former case there is no such excuse - because the life of a people will again be at stake in the future." **-Captain Sir Basil Liddell Hart**

"Let a man lay his plans with due regard to common sense, and he will usually succeed." **-Themistocles**

"Of course, with the increasing number of aeroplanes one gains increased opportunities for shooting down one's enemies, but at the same time, the possibility of being shot down one's self increases." **-Manfred von Richthofen**

"Spies cannot be usefully employed without a certain intuitive sagacity. They cannot be properly managed without benevolence and straightforwardness. Without subtle ingenuity of mind, one cannot make certain of the truth of their reports. Be subtle! Be subtle! And use your spies for every kind of business." **-Sun Tzu**

"On the Spartan side, it was a memorable fight; they were men who understood war pitted against an inexperienced enemy, and amongst the feints they employed was to turn their backs in a body and pretend to be retreating in confusion, whereupon the enemy would come on with a great clatter and roar, supposing the battle won; but the Spartans, just as the Persians were on them, would wheel and face them, and inflict in the struggle innumerable casualties." **-Greek historian Herodotus, describing the battle of Thermopylae.**

"Marriage for young warriors is a folly. Their first and last duty is to protect the nation from its enemies. This they cannot do efficiently if they have family ties... I tell you all, in future a man will have to prove his worth to be a father, before he receives permission to marry." -**Shaka Zulu**

"Marriage is good for nothing in the military profession." -**Napoleon Bonaparte**

"It is better to beat the enemy through want, surprises, and care for difficult places (i.e., through manoeuvre) than by a battle in the open field."
-**Publius Flavius Vegetius Renatus**

"It is essential to know the character of the enemy and of their principal officers - whether they be rash or cautious, enterprising or timid, whether they fight on principle or from chance." -**Publius Flavius Vegetius Renatus**

"Stand your guard.  Don't fire unless fired upon, but if they mean to have a war, let it begin here." -**Captain John Parker**

"If we are outnumbered, concentrate our troops and keep on attacking the enemy. Then even though he is numerous, he can be forced to submit." -**Wu Qi**

"Leaping is another very necessary exercise, to enable them to pass ditches or embarrassing eminences of any kind without trouble or difficulty. There is also another very material advantage to be derived from these exercises in time of action; for a soldier who advances with his javelin, running and leaping, dazzles the eyes of his adversary, strikes him with terror, and gives him the fatal stroke before he has time to put himself on his defense." -**Publius Flavius Vegetius Renatus**

"The art of war is divided between art and strategem. What cannot be done by force, must be done my strategem." -**Frederick the Great**

"When you go into the country hawking, you learn to understand the military spirit and also the hard life of the lower classes. You exercise your muscles and train your limbs. You have any amount of walking and running and become quite indifferent to heat and cold, and so you are little likely to suffer from any illness." -**Tokugawa Ieyasu**

"Don't fire until you see the whites of their eyes!" -**Col. William Prescott**

"Projects of absolute defense are not practicable because while seeking to place yourself in strong camps the enemy will envelop you, deprive you of your supplies from the rear and oblige you to lose ground, thus disheartening your troops. Hence, I prefer to this conduct the temerity of the offensive with the hazard of losing the battle since this will not be more fatal than retreat and timid defensive. In the one case you lose ground by withdrawing and soldiers by desertion and you have no hope; in the other you do not risk more and, if you are fortunate, you can hope for the most brilliant success."
-**Frederick the Great**

"Victory resulted from his cunning strategy rather than the bravery of his troops."
-**Julius Caesar**

"The main and principal point in war is to secure plenty of provisions for oneself and to destroy the enemy by famine. Famine is more terrible than the sword."
-**Publius Flavius Vegetius Renatus**

"To place any dependence upon militia is, assuredly, resting upon a broken staff. Men just dragged from the tender scenes of domestic life, unaccustomed to the din of arms; totally unacquainted with every kind of military skill, which being followed by a want of confidence in themselves, when opposed to troops regularly trained, disciplined and appointed, makes them timid and ready to fly from their own shadows."
-**George Washington**

"It is no easy matter to train the horse or foot archer, or to form the legionary soldier to every part of the drill, to teach him not to quit his post, to keep ranks, to take a proper aim and throw his missile weapons with force, to dig trenches, to plant palisades, how to manage his shield, glance off the blows of the enemy, and how to parry a stroke with dexterity. A soldier, thus perfect in his business, so far from showing any backwardness to engage, will be eager for an opportunity of signaling himself."
**-Publius Flavius Vegetius Renatus**

"In case signals can neither be seen nor perfectly understood, no captain can do very wrong if he places his ship alongside that of the enemy." **-Horatio Nelson**

"Engage the enemy more closely." **-Horatio Nelson**

"If it is to your advantage, make a forward move; if not, stay where you are."
**-Sun Tzu**

"Get there first with the most men." **-Attributed to General Nathan Bedford Forrest**

"To make these dispositions is not hard; the difficulty is to discover a body of men who will dash forward and charge an enemy as above described intelligently and loyally, with an eager spirit and unfailing courage." **-Xenophon**

"In war, you must be prepared for what is possible, not only what is probable."
**-Robert Baden-Powell**

"If you have to sleep on hard ground, the secret of comfort is to scoop out a little hole, about the size of a teacup, where your hip-bone will rest.  It makes all the difference..."
**-Robert Baden-Powell**

"The greatest harm can befall the army is a result of hesitation." -**Wu Qi**

"Whether we go or stay... there is no real difficulty, if only we agree on one course of action; but if we go on quarrelling, there is no chance of escape." **-Julius Caesar, reporting the words of the centurion Sabinus.**

"The thing is to look out for every chance and seize it – run at it and jump on it – don't sit down and wait for it to pass. Opportunity is a bus which has very few stopping places." -**Robert Baden-Powell**

"But in any attempt to attack superior forces, in full certainty that, do what you can, you must eventually retire, it is far better, say I, under these circumstances to bring a fraction only of your whole force into action, which fraction should be the pick and flower of the troops at your command, both horses and men. A body of that size and quality will be able to strike a blow and to fall back with greater security." -**Xenophon**

"All that is advantageous to the enemy is disadvantageous to you, and all that is useful to you, damages the enemy." -**Publius Flavius Vegetius Renatus**

"Time and opportunity may help to retrieve other misfortunes, but where forage and provisions have not been carefully provided, the evil is without remedy."
-**Publius Flavius Vegetius Renatus**

"If the soldiers are committed to fighting to death, they will live; if they seek to stay alive, they will die." -**Wu Qi**

Do not interfere with an army that is returning home. When you surround an army, leave an outlet free. Do not press a desperate foe too hard. Such is the art of warfare."
-**Sun Tzu**

"It is a military axiom not to advance uphill against the enemy, nor to oppose him when he comes downhill. Do not pursue an enemy who simulates flight; do not attack soldiers whose temper is keen. Do not swallow bait offered by the enemy." -**Maxims of Sun Tzu**

"Just because we have won victory, we must never relax our vigilance." -**Mao Zedong**

"A battle plan is good only until enemy contact is made. From then on, your ability to execute the plan depends on what the enemy does. If your assess-ment of the enemy is good, then you probably have anticipated his actions or reactions and will be able to quickly develop or adjust your plan accordingly. If your assessment is bad, due to poor understanding of how the enemy fights or poor battlefield intelligence, then you will probably get surprised, react slowly, lose the initiative, and cause your unit to be defeated." -**General Norman Schwarzkopf**

"The general who is skilled in defense hides in the most secret recesses of the earth; he who is skilled in attack flashes forth from the topmost heights of heaven. Thus on the one hand we have ability to protect ourselves; on the other, a victory is complete."
-**Sun Tzu**

"Now, my maxim would be precisely converse: if you attack with a prospect of superiority, do not grudge employing all the power at your command; excess of victory never yet caused any conqueror one pang of remorse." -**Xenophon**

"There is another precaution which I feel called upon to note. Some generals, in attacking a force which they imagine to be inferior to their own, will advance with a ridiculously insufficient force, so that it is the merest accident if they do not experience the injury they were minded to inflict. Conversely, in attacking any enemy whose superiority is a well-known fact, they will bring the whole of their force into action."
-**Xenophon**

"Do not repeat the tactics which have gained you one victory, but let your methods be regulated by the infinite variety of circumstances." -**Sun Tzu**

"The art of war teaches us to rely not on the likelihood of the enemy's not coming, but on our own readiness to receive him; not on the chance of his not attacking, but rather on the fact that we have made our position unassailable." -**Sun Tzu**

"There is a need to win the minds of the valiant, sharing their likes and dislikes. Only after this, the stratagems should be used. Without stratagems, you have no means to resolve suspicion and settle doubts. Without being scheming and unorthodox, you have no means to destroy evildoers. Without plotting, there is no means to be successful." -**Huang Shi Gong**

"It is better to have several bodies of reserves than to extend your front too much. A general is not easily overcome who can form a true judgment of his own and the enemy's forces. Valor is superior to numbers. The nature of the ground is often of more consequence than courage. Few men are born brave; many become so through care and force of discipline. An army is strengthened by labor and enervated by idleness. Troops are not to be led to battle unless confident of success. Novelty and surprise throw an enemy into consternation; but common incidents have no effect. He who rashly pursues a flying enemy with troops in disorder, seems inclined to resign that victory which he had before obtained. An army unsupplied with grain and other necessary provisions will be vanquished without striking a blow." -**Maxims of Publius Flavius Vegetius Renatus**

"A general in all of his projects should not think so much about what he wishes to do as what his enemy will do; that he should never underestimate this enemy, but he should put himself in his place to appreciate difficulties and hindrances the enemy could not interpose; that his plans will be deranged at the slightest event if he has not foreseen everything and if he has not devised means with which to surmount the obstacles." -**Frederick the Great**

"Strategy is a system of makeshifts. It is more than a science, it is the application of science to practical affairs; it is carrying through an originally conceived plan under a constantly shifting set of circumstances. It is the art of acting under the pressure of the most difficult kind of conditions. Strategy is the application of common sense in the work of leading an army; its teachings hardly go beyond the first requirement of common sense; its value lies entirely in its concrete application. It is a matter of understanding correctly at every moment a constantly changing situation, and then doing the simplest and most natural thing with energy and determination. This is what makes war an art, an art that is served by many sciences. Like every art, war cannot be learned rationally, but only by experience. In war, as in art, there can be no set standards nor can code of rules take the place of brains." **-Field Marshal Helmuth Graf von Moltke**

"In general, the way to command a marching army is to not contravene the proper timing advancing and stopping; not miss the appropriate times for eating and drinking; and not completely exhaust the strength of the men and horses." **-Wu Qi**

"But now suppose that a commander, aftermaking a feint in this style, presently on wheeling quickens for the charge and quickens to retire – he will be able to hit the enemy far harder, and pull through absolutely without scathing himself." **-Xenophon**

"Here, too, is a maxim to engrave upon the memory: in charging a superior force, never to leave a difficult tract of ground in the rear of your attack, since there is all the difference in the world between a stumble in flight and a stumble in pursuit."
**-Xenophon**

"The commander who has won the sovereign's trust and has an independent command will win. The one who knows the art of war will win. The one who gets uniform support from his soldiers will win. The one whose subordinates work in concert with each other will win. The one who is good at analyzing and utilizing terrain will win."
**-Sun Bin**

"Severity of toil weighs nothing in the scale against the danger of engaging a force superior to your own. Still, if on any occasion the enemy advance in any way to place himself between fortified points that are friendly to you, let him be never so superior in force, your game is to attack on whichever flank you can best conceal your advance, or, still better, on both flanks simultaneously; since, while one detachment is retiring after delivering its attack, a charge pressed home from the opposite quarter cannot fail to throw the enemy into confusion and to give safety to your friends." -**Xenophon**

"Do not assume that having the numerical advantage, we can treat the enemy lightly." -**Jiang Taigong**

"At times there is no more effective fraud than a make-believe of over-caution alien to the spirit of adventure. This itself will put the enemy off his guard and ten to one will lure him into some egregious blunder; or conversely, once get a reputation for foolhardiness established, and then with folded hands sit feigning future action, and see what a world of trouble you will thereby cause your adversary." -**Xenophon**

"An army marches on its stomach." -**Attributed to Napoleon**

"Our strategy in going after this army is very simple. First we are going to cut it off, and then we are going to kill it." -**Colin Powell**

"There are no secrets to success. It is the result of preparation, hard work and learning from failure." -**Colin Powell**

"In short, absolute, so-called mathematical factors never find a firm basis in military calculations. From the very start there is an interplay of possibilities, probabilities, good luck and bad that weaves its way throughout the length and breadth of the tapestry. In the whole range of human activities, war most closely resembles a game of cards." -**Karl von Clausewitz**

"Nothing is more worthy of the attention of a good general than the endeavour to penetrate the designs of the enemy." -**Machiavelli**

"For every one must confess that there is no greater proof of the abilities of a general than to investigate, with the utmost care, into the character and natural abilities of his opponent." -**Polybius**

"It is always proper to assume that the enemy will do what he should do."
-**Robert E. Lee**

"There is always hazard in military movements, but we must decide between the possible loss of inaction and the risk of action." -**Robert E. Lee**

"To fail to think fast when surrounded by the enemy is to have your back pressed to the wall; And to fail to take the battle to the enemy when your back is to the wall is to perish." -**Sun Tzu**

"Battles are won by superiority of fire." -**Frederick the Great**

"I know well that war is a great evil and the worst of all evils. But since our enemies clearly look upon the shedding of blood as one of their basic duties and the height of virtue, and since each one must stand up for his country and his own people with word, pen, and deed, we have decided to write about strategy. But putting it into practice we shall be able not only to resist our enemies but even to conquer them... Strategy is the means by which a commander may defend his own lands and defeat his enemies. The general is the one who practices strategy." -**Anonymous Byzantine General**

"In order to smash, it is necessary to act suddenly." -**Napoleon Bonaparte**

"To ensure that your whole host may withstand the brunt of the enemy's attack and remain unshaken - this is effected by maneuvers direct and indirect.

That the impact of your army may be like a grindstone dashed against an egg - that is effected by science of weak and strong points.

In all fighting, the direct methods may be used for joining battle, but indirect methods will be needed in order to secure victory.

Indirect tactics, efficiently applied, are inexhaustable as Heaven and Earth, unending as the flow of rivers and streams; like the sun and moon, they end but to begin anew; like the four seasons, they pass but to return once more.

There are not more than five musical notes, yet the combinations of these five give rise to more melodies than can ever be heard. There are not more than five primary colors, yet in combination they produce more hues than can ever be seen. There are not more than five cardinal tastes, yet combinations of them yield more flavours than can ever be tasted.

In battle, there are not more than two methods of attack - the direct and indirect; yet these two in combination give rise to an endless series of maneuvers. The direct and indirect lead on to each other in turn. It is like moving in a circle - you never come to an end. Who can exhaust the possibilities of their combinations?" -**Sun Tzu**


"It is better to avoid a tricky opponent than one who never lets up. The latter makes no secret of what he is doing, whereas it is difficult to find out what the other is up to."
-**The Emperor Maurice**


"The one great element in continuing the success of an offensive is maintaining the momentum." -**George Marshall**


"War is an art and as such is not susceptible of explanation by fixed formula."
-**General Patton**

"In war one sees his own troubles and not those of the enemy." -**Napoleon Bonaparte**

"The measure may be thought bold, but I am of the opinion the boldest are the safest." -**Horatio Nelson to Sir Hyde Parker urging vigorous action against the Russians and Danes.**

"Follow a defeated enemy ruthlessly and put the fear of Shaka into him." -**Shaka Zulu**

"Battles are won by slaughter and manoeuvre. The greater the general, the more he contributes to the manoeuvre, the less he demands in slaughter." -**Winston Churchill**

"Strategy is the determination of the direction of the main blow - The plan of strategy is the plan of the organization of the decisive blow in the direction in which the blow can most quickly give the maximum results.

In other words, to define the direction of the main blow means to predetermine the nature of operations in the whole period of war, to determine nine-tenths of the fate of the entire war. In this is the main task of strategy." -**Joseph Stalin**

"They approach like foxes, fight like lions, and disappear like birds." -**European settler describing American Indian raids.**

"Three men behind the enemy are worth more than fifty in front of him." -**Frederick the Great**

"Use steamroller strategy; that is, make up your mind on course and direction of action, and stick to it. But in tactics, do not steamroller. Attack weakness. Hold them by the nose and kick them in the pants." -**General Patton**

"Hence the saying: If you know the enemy and know yourself, you need not fear the result of a hundred battles. If you know yourself but not the enemy, for every victory gained you will also suffer a defeat. If you know neither the enemy nor yourself, you will succumb in every battle." -**Sun Tzu**

"Country in which there are precipitous cliffs with torrents running between, deep natural hollows, confined places, tangled thickets, quagmires and crevasses, should be left with all possible speed and not approached.

While we keep away from such places, we should get the enemy to approach them; while we face them, we should let the enemy have them on his rear."-**Sun Tzu**

"It is also greatly in the commander's own interest to have a personal picture of the front and a clear idea of the problems his subordinates are having to face. It is the only way in which he can keep his ideas permanently up to date and adapted to changing conditions. If he fights his battles as a game of chess, he will become rigidly fixed in academic theory and admiration of his own ideas. Success comes most readily to the commander whose ideas have not been canalised into any one fixed channel, but can develop freely from the conditions around him." -**Erwin Rommel**

"I was too weak to defend, so I attacked." -**Robert E. Lee**

"Battles decide the fate of a nation. In war it is absolutely necessary to come to decisive actions either to get out of the distress of war or to place the enemy in that position, or even to settle a quarrel which otherwise perhaps would never be finished. A wise man will make no movement without good reason, and a general of an army will never give battle if it does not serve some important purpose. When he is forced by his enemy into battle it is surely because he will have committed mistakes which force him to dance to the tune of his enemy." -**Frederick the Great**

"What is the concept of defense? The parrying of a blow. What is its characteristic feature? awaiting the blow. It is this feature which turns any action into a defensive one; it is the only test by which defense can be distinguished from attack in war. Pure defense, however, would be completely contrary to the idea of war, since it would mean that only one side was waging it... But if we are really waging war, we must return the enemy's blows; and these offensive acts in a defensive war come under the heading of 'defense' - in other words, our offensive takes place within our own positions or theater of operations. Thus, a defensive campaign can be fought with offensive battles, and in a defensive battle, we can employ our divisions offensively. Even in a defensive position awaiting the enemy assault, our bullets take the offensive. So the defensive form of war is not a simple shield, but a shield made up of well-directed blows."
**-Karl von Clausewitz**

"Always mystify, mislead, and surprise the enemy, if possible; and when you strike and overcome him, never give up the pursuit as long as your men have strength to follow; for an army routed, if hotly pursued, becomes panic-stricken, and can then be destroyed by half their number." **-Stonewall Jackson**

"The young recruits in particular must be exercised in running, in order to charge the enemy with vigor, to occupy on occasion an advantageous post with greater expedition, and balk the enemy in their designs upon the same; and that they may, when sent to reconnoiter, advance with speed, and return with celerity and more easily overtake the enemy in pursuit." **-Flavius Vegetius Renatus**

"Great advantage is drawn from knowledge of your adversary, and when you know the measure of his intelligence and character you can use it to play on his weaknesses."
**-Frederick the Great**

"In war it is not numbers that give the advantage. If you do not advance recklessly, and are able to consolidate your own strength, get a clear picture of the enemy's situation, and secure the full support of your men, it is enough." **-Sun Tzu**

"In reviewing the whole array of factors a general must weigh before making his decision, we must remember that he can gauge the direction and value of the most important ones only by considering numerous other possibilities - some immediate, some remote. He must guess, so, to speak: guess whether the first shock of battle will steel the enemy's resolve and stiffen his resistance, or whether, like a Bologna flask, it will shatter as soon as its surface is scratched; guess the extent of debilitation and paralysis that the drying up of particular sources of supply and the severing of certain lines of communication will cause in the enemy; guess whether the burning pain of an injury he has dealt will make the enemy collapse with exhaustion or, like a wounded bull, arouse his rage; guess whether the other powers will be frightened or indignant, and whether and which political alliances will be dissolved or formed. When we realize that he must hit upon all this and much more by means of his discreet judgment, as a marksman hits a target, we must admit that such an accomplishment of the human mind is no small achievement. Thousands of wrong turns running in all directions tempt his perception; and if the range, confusion and complexity of the issues are not enough to overwhelm him, the dangers and responsibilities may." -**Karl von Clausewitz**

"The whole art of war consists in a well reasoned and extremely circumspect defensive, followed by rapid and audacious attack." -**Napoleon Bonaparte**

"The most difficult thing is to discern the enemy's plans, and to detect the truth in all reports one receives: the remainder requires only common sense."
-**Napoleon Bonaparte**

"Forward, even with only a spear." -**Samurai Proverb**

"Troops defeated in open battle should not be pampered or, even if it seems like a good idea, take refuge in a fortified camp or some other strong place, but while their fear is still fresh, they should attack again. By not indulging them they may with greater assurance renew the fighting." -**The Emperor Maurice**

"When you engage in actual fighting, if victory is long in coming, the men's weapons will grow dull and their ardour will be damped. If you lay siege to a town, you will exhaust your strength. Again, if the campaign is protracted, the resources of the State will not be equal to the strain.

Now, when your weapons are dulled, your ardour damped, your strength exhausted and your treasure spent, other chieftains will spring up to take advantage of your extremity. Then no man, however wise, will be able to avert the consequences that must ensue.

Thus, though we have heard of stupid haste in war, cleverness has never been associated with long delays. There is no instance of a country having been benefited by a prolonged war." -**Sun Tzu**

# Chapter 5
# Honor

*A* warrior is trained to kill people. This truth may sound brutal, but it is a fact. But what is it that allows one man to kill another in war and still be the hero we all admire? Why was Rommel treated with respect and admired by those he fought against, whereas the other German leaders during World War II were thought of as nefarious and violent criminals? What was the crucial difference between Saladin and Saddam Hussein? It was honor – with its strict sense of right and wrong, and a high level of personal integrity and morality—that redeems human actions. This sense of honor works alongside courage to help a warrior face danger and will inspire courage even when other motives have weakened.

*Honor also inspires the warrior to protect the weak and not use strength to oppress others. Thus honor combines a range of virtues with courage, like mercy and justice. All cultures have upheld the model of chivalry as an ideal – strength protecting weakness by fighting against evil. And honor is linked closely with duty as well as courage: honor tells a warrior what is right and what is wrong while duty prompts the warrior to act in a way that is right, and courage gives the warrior the ability to do what is right no matter what the danger.*

---

"I love the name of honor more than I fear death." **-Julius Caesar**

"One obtains everything from men by appealing to their sense of honour."
**-Napoleon Bonaparte**

"The best memorial for a mighty man is to gain honour ere death." **-Beowulf**

"Let men decide firmly what they will not do, and they will be free to do vigorously what they ought to do." -**Mencius**

"Do what is right, not what you think the high headquarters wants or what you think will make you look good." -**General Norman Schwarzkopf**

"Marine Corps integrity is doing that thing which is right, when no one is looking." -**Col. Colin Lampard**

"The truth of the matter is that you always know the right thing to do. The hard part is doing it." -**General Norman Schwarzkopf**

"Do not act as if thou wert going to live ten thousand years. Death hangs over thee. While thou livest, while it is in thy power, be good." -**Marcus Aurelius**

"Let us raise a standard to which the wise and honest can repair; the rest is in the hands of God." -**George Washington**

"How much trouble he avoids who does not look to see what his neighbour says or does or thinks, but only to what he does himself, that it may be just and pure; or, as Agathon says, look not round at the depraved morals of others, but run straight along the line without deviating from it." -**Marcus Aurelius**

"When the proper form of propriety is observed, the wise officers will come." -**Huang Shi Gong**

"Do thou therefore I say absolutely and freely make choice of that which is best, and stick unto it." -**Marcus Aurelius**

"Labor to keep alive in your breast that little spark of celestial fire, called conscience."
**-George Washington**

"If you dismiss one good man, then all good people will lose heart. Reward an evil person and all evil persons will be drawn to you." **-Huang Shi Gong**

"Do not be whirled about, but in every movement have respect to justice."
**-Marcus Aurelius**

"Associate yourself with men of good quality if you esteem your own reputation. It is better be alone than in bad company." **-George Washington**

"Duty is the most sublime word in our language. Do your duty in all things. You cannot do more. You should never wish to do less." **-Robert E. Lee**

"Let these officers but be persuaded that from the public point of view, the splendid appearance of their squadrons will confer a title to distinction far higher than that of any personal equipment. Nor is it reasonable to suppose that they will be deaf to such an argument, since the very desire to hold the office of phylarch [captain of a division] itself proclaims a soul alive to honour and ambition." **-Xenophon**

"Never esteem of anything as profitable, which shall ever constrain thee either to break thy faith." **-Marcus Aurelius**

"I think it better to do right, even if we suffer in so doing, than to incur the reproach of our consciences and posterity." **-Robert E. Lee**

"If any man is able to convince me and show me that I do not think or act rightly, I will gladly change; for I seek the truth, by which no man was ever injured. But he is injured who abides in his error and ignorance." -**Marcus Aurelius**

"Nothing does so much honor to the abilities or application of the tribune as the appearance and discipline of the soldiers, when their apparel is neat and clean, their arms bright and in good order and when they perform their exercises and evolutions with dexterity." -**Publius Flavius Vegetius Renatus**

"Never value anything as profitable to thyself which shall compel thee to break thy promise." -**Marcus Aurelius**

"The trite saying that honesty is the best policy has met with the just criticism that honesty is not policy. The real honest man is honest from conviction of what is right, not from policy." -**Robert E. Lee**

"Whoever prefers death to ignominity will save his life and live in honour, but he who prefers life will die and cover himself with disgrace." -**Napoleon Bonaparte**

"Another may be more expert in casting his opponent; but he is not more social, nor more modest, nor better disciplined to meet all that happens, nor more considerate with respect to the faults of his neighbors." -**Marcus Aurelius**

"Pure, incorruptible officers cannot be enticed with rank and salary. Self-constrained, righteous officers cannot be coerced with threats." -**Huang Shi Gong**

"Use thine opinative faculty with all honour and respect, for in her indeed is all."
-**Marcus Aurelius**

"You must study to be frank with the world: frankness is the child of honesty and courage. Say just what you mean to do on every occasion, and take it for granted that you mean to do right." -**Robert E. Lee**

"What constitute officers are men of valor and character. Thus it is said that if you remove men of valor and character from enemy states, they will be impoverished."
-**Huang Shi Gong**

"Whatever any one does or says, I must be good; just as if the gold, or the emerald, or the purple were always saying this: Whatever any one does or says, I must be emerald and keep my color." -**Marcus Aurelius**

"Labor disgraces no man; unfortunately, you occasionally find men who disgrace labor."
-**Ulysses S. Grant**

"Death hangs over thee: whilst yet thou livest, whilst thou mayest, be good."
-**Marcus Aurelius**

"No personal consideration should stand in the way of performing a public duty."
-**Ulysses S. Grant**

"Mark the blameless man and observe the upright; for the future of that man is peace."
-**King David**

"Thus choosing to die resisting, rather than to live submitting, they fled only from dishonour, but met danger face to face, and after one brief moment, while at the summit of their fortune, left be-hind them not their fear, but their glory." -**Pericles' funeral oration for the Athenian soldiers.**

"For if any man should conceive certain things as being really good, such as prudence, temperance, justice, fortitude, he would not after having first conceived these endure to listen to anything which should not be in harmony with what is really good."
**-Marcus Aurelius**

"If the general refuses to ask and listen to advice, then those that are capable will leave. If he refuse to take into consideration any plans set out by strategists, the strategists will leave. If good and evil are treated alike, the meritorious will grow weary. If the general is stubborn, his subordinates will shirk all responsibility. If he brags, his assistants will not attempt any accomplishments. If he believes slander, he will lose the hearts of the people. If he is greedy, treachery will be unchecked. If he is licentious, his officers and men will follow suit. If the general has one of the faults mentioned here, the masses will not submit. If he has two of them, the army will lack discipline. If he has three of them, his subordinates will not fight. If he has four of them, the entire state is in danger."
**-Huang Shi Gong**

"Judge every word and deed which are according to nature to be fit for thee; and be not diverted by the blame which follows from any people nor by their words, but if a thing is good to be done or said, do not consider it unworthy of thee." **-Marcus Aurelius**

"Last, but by no means least, courage of one's convictions, the courage to see things through. The world is in a constant conspiracy against the brave. It's the age-old struggle: the roar of the crowd on one side and the voice of your conscience on the other." **-Douglas MacArthur**

"To comprehend all in a few words, our life is short; we must endeavour to gain the present time with best discretion and justice." **-Marcus Aurelius**

"Only those are fit to live who are not afraid to die." **-Douglas MacArthur**

"Duty, Honor, Country. Those three hallowed words reverently dictate what you ought to be, what you can be, what you will be. They are your rallying point to build courage when courage seems to fail, to regain faith when there seems to be little cause for faith, to create hope when hope becomes forlorn" -**Douglas MacArthur**

"The soul is dyed by the thoughts." -**Marcus Aurelius**

"War must be carried on systematically, and to do it you must have men of character activated by principles of honor." -**George Washington**

"A man does what he must.. in spite of personal consequences, in spite of obstacles and dangers, and pressures.. and that is the basis of all human morality." -**John F Kennedy**

"Great ambition is the passion of a great character. Those endowed with it may perform very good or very bad acts. All depends on the principles which direct them."
-**Napoleon Bonaparte**

"Moral courage is the most valuable and usually the most absent characteristic in men."
-**General Patton**

"Keep thyself then simple, good, pure, serious, free from affectation, a friend of justice, a worshipper of the gods, kind, affectionate, strenuous in all proper acts."
-**Marcus Aurelius**

"I am not carrying on a war of extermination against the Romans. I am contending for honor and empire. My ancestors yielded to Roman valour. I am endeavouring that others, in their turn, will be obliged to yield to my good fortune, and my valour."
-**Hannibal**

"Unless you do your best, the day will come when, tired and hungry, you will halt just short of the goal you were ordered to reach, and by halting you will make useless the efforts and deaths of thousands." **-General Patton**

"The perfection of moral character consists in this, in passing every day as the last, and in being neither violently excited nor torpid nor playing the hypocrite."
**-Marcus Aurelius**

"Character... is a habit, the daily choice of right over wrong; it is a moral quality which grows to maturity in peace and is not suddenly developed on the outbreak of war."
 **-Lord Moran**

"Only attend to thyself, and resolve to be a good man in every act which thou dost."
**-Marcus Aurelius**

"The first and last essential of an efficient soldier is character; without it he will not long endure the perils of modern war." **-Lord Moran**

"Waste no more time arguing what a good man should be.  Be one."  **-Marcus Aurelius**

"What is the use of living if it is not to strive for noble causes and to make this muddled world a better place for those who will live in it after we are gone?"
**-Winston Churchill**

"It would be a man's happiest lot to depart from mankind without having had any taste of lying and hypocrisy and luxury and pride." **-Marcus Aurelius**

"The probability that we might fail in the struggle ought not to deter us from the support of a cause we believe to be just." **-Abraham Lincoln**

"Let us therefore brace ourselves to our duty, and so bear ourselves that, if the British Empire and its Commonwealth lasts for a thousand years, men will still say, 'This was their finest hour." **-Winston Churchill**

"A military man can scarcely pride himself on having 'smitten a sleeping enemy'; in fact, to have it pointed out is more a matter of shame." **-Admiral Isoroku Yamamoto**

"Nothing will stand in the way of thy acting justly and soberly and considerately." **-Marcus Aurelius**

"I did not undertake the war for private ends, but in the cause of national liberty." **-Vercingetorix**

"Look at the best knight that you have ever seen… he is brave and courtly and skilful, and noble and of good lineage and eloquent…his wealth was never denied to any, but each has as much as he wants…and he has never been slow to perform honorable deeds. He dearly loves God and the Trinity… he has honored the poor and lowly; and he judges each according to his worth." **-Anonymous writer of the medieval work *Girart,* describing an ideal knight.**

"In every pain let this thought be present: that there is no dishonour in it." **-Marcus Aurelius**

"Thy necessity is yet greater than mine." **-Last words of Sir Philip Sydney, passing his drink to a poor soldier.**

"In his youth, a man should use without laziness or delay his prowess, his valor, and the strength of his body for the honor and profit of himself and his dependants; for he who passes his youth without exploit may have cause for great shame and grief. The young nobleman, knight or man-at-arms could work to acquire honor, to be renowned for bravery, and to have temporal possessions, riches and heritages on which he can live honorably." -**Philippe de Navarre**

"Here is what prudence dictates: put yourself in a position where you fear neither your friends nor your enemies, but when you make a treaty, stick to your word."
-**Frederick the Great**

"One does not employ righteous officers using solely material wealth. This is because the Righteous will not die for the malevolent." -**Huang Shi Gong**

"Your fathers worked hard, fought hard and died hard to make this Empire for you. Don't let them look down from heaven and see you loafing about with hands in your pockets doing nothing to keep it up." -**Robert Baden-Powell**

"As the action was taking place in full view of everyone, no gallant exploit and no act of cowardice could pass unnoticed, the thirst for glory and the fear of disgrace was an incentive to both sides." -**Julius Caesar**

"Always be ready, with your armor on, except when you are taking your rest at night. At whatever you are working, try to win honor and a name for honesty. Defend the poor and weak. Help them who cannot defend themselves. Do nothing to hurt or offend anyone else. Be prepared to fight in the defense of their country. Work for honor rather than profit. Never break your promise. Maintain the honor of your country with your life. Rather die honestly than live shamefully." -**The code of chivalry, according to Robert Baden-Powell.**

"The knights considered their honor their most sacred possession. They would not do a dishonorable thing such as telling a lie or stealing. They would rather die than do it. They were always ready to fight and be killed in upholding their king, or their religion, or their honor... the knight's patrol used to stick to him through thick and thin, and all carried out the same idea as their leader, namely: their honor was sacred; they were loyal to God, their king and their country; they were particularly courteous and polite to all women and children, and weak people; they were helpful to everybody; they gave money and food where it was needed, and saved up their money to do so; they taught themselves the use of arms in order to protect their religion and their country against enemies; they kept themselves healthy and active in order to be able to do these things well. You... cannot do better than follow the example of the knights."
**-Robert Baden-Powell**

"When evil men of courage praise each other, they cover the ruler's eyes and confuse his wisdom. When both slander and praise arise together, they block the ruler's ears, making unable to discern good and bad. When they praise and cover each other, the ruler will lose the loyal." **-Huang Shi Gong**

"The soldier's trade, if it is to mean anything at all, has to be anchored to an unshakeable code of honor. Otherwise, those of us who follow the drums become nothing more than a bunch of hired assassins walking around in gaudy clothes... a disgrace to God and mankind." **-Karl von Clausewitz**

"I would lay down my life for America, but I cannot trifle with my honor."
**-Admiral John Paul Jones**

"God forbid that I should do this thing, and flee away from them: if our time be come, let us die manfully for our brethren, and let us not stain our honour." **-Judas Maccabeus**

"When deceitful ministers hold superior positions, the entire army will be clamoring and contentious." **-Huang Shi Gong**

"Suppose that men kill thee, cut thee in pieces, curse thee. What then can these things do to prevent thy mind from remaining pure, wise, sober, just? For instance, if a man should stand by a limpid pure spring, and curse it, the spring never ceases sending up potable water; and if he should cast clay into it or filth, it will speedily disperse them and wash them out, and will not be at all polluted. How then shalt thou possess a perpetual fountain and not a mere well? By forming thyself hourly to freedom conjoined with contentment, simplicity, and modesty." -**Marcus Aurelius**

"What is life without honor? Degradation is worse than death. We must think of the living and of those who are come after us, and see that with God's blessing we transmit to them the freedom we have ourselves inherited." -**Stonewall Jackson**

"War creates such a strain that all the pettiness, jealousy, ambition and greed, and selfishness begin to leak out of the seams of the average character. On top of this are the problems created by the enemy." -**Dwight D. Eisenhower**

"Every post is honorable in which a man can serve his country." -**George Washington**

"Judge me, O LORD; for I have walked in mine integrity: I have trusted also in the LORD; therefore I shall not slide. Examine me, O LORD, and prove me; try my reins and my heart. For thy lovingkindness is before mine eyes: and I have walked in thy truth. I have not sat with vain persons, neither will I go in with dissemblers. I have hated the congregation of evil doers; and will not sit with the wicked." -***King David***

"I would sacrifice Gwalior, or every frontier of India, ten times over, in order to preserve our credit for scrupulous good faith, and the advan-tages and honor we gained by the late war and the peace; and we must not fritter them away in arguments, drawn from over-strained principles of the laws of nations, which are not under-stood in this country. What brought me through many difficulties in the war, and the negotiations for peace? The British good faith, and nothing else." -**Sir Arthur Wellesley, The Duke of Wellington**

"It is satisfaction to a man to do the proper works of a man. Now it is a proper work of a man to be benevolent to his own kind." -**Marcus Aurelius**

"My character and good name are in my own keeping. Life with disgrace is dreadful. A glorious death is to be envied." -**Horatio Nelson**

"In honour I gained them, and in honour I will die with them." -**Horatio Nelson, when asked to cover the stars on his uniform to hide his rank during battle.**

"Commanders must have integrity; without integrity, they have no power. If they have no power, they cannot bring out the best in their armies. Therefore, integrity is the hand of warriorship." -**Sun Bin**

"No nation can safely trust its martial honor to leaders who do not maintain the universal code which distinguishes between those things that are right and those things that are wrong." -**Douglas MacArthur**

"Never give in, never give in, never, never, never - in nothing great or small, large or petty - never give in except in convictions of honour and good sense."
-**Winston Churchill**

"When asked why the best men prefer an honourable death to a life without honour, he said: 'Because they regard the latter as the gift of Nature, and the former as being in their own hands.'" -**King Leonidas of Sparta**

# Chapter 6
# Self-Control & Perseverance

*W*e all know that warriors are both physically and mentally tough. Warriors have to be highly disciplined so these strengths create the motives and incumbent acts of duty, to face dangers that would drive lesser human beings asunder. This virtue, known to the ancients as Fortitude, requires a tough mind and a tough body. Self-control and self- discipline, however, require more than just the bulldog spirit of never quitting. Self-control demands also that a warrior doesn't give into the temptations that honor forbids, whether those temptations result in inhuman acts or a self-seeking indulgence for luxuries.

---

"There is nothing more base than for a man to lose his temper too often. No matter how angry one becomes, his first thought should be to pacify his mind and come to a clear understanding of the situation at hand. Then, if he is in the right, to become angry is correct." **-Shiba Yoshimasa**

"Every duty is a charge, but the charge of oneself is the root of all others." **-Mencius**

"For where there is no one in control nothing useful or distinguished can be done. This is roughly true of all departments of life, and entirely true where soldiering is concerned. Here it is discipline that makes one feel safe, while lack of discipline has destroyed many people before now." **-Xenophon**

"When you get to the end of your rope, tie a knot and hang on."
**-Franklin D. Roosevelt**

"You pick out the big men! I'll make them brave." -**Pyrrhus**

"Life is like unto a long journey with a heavy burden. Let thy step be slow and steady, that thou stumble not. Persuade thyself that imperfection and inconvenience are the natural lot of mortals, and there will be no room for discontent, neither for despair. When ambitious desires arise in thy heart, recall the days of extremity thou has passed through. Forbearance is the root of quietness and assurance forever. Look upon the wrath of the enemy. If thou knowest only what it is to conquer, and knowest not what it is to be defeated, woe unto thee; it will fare ill with thee. Find fault with thyself rather than with others." -**Tokugawa Ieyasu**

"Let it make no difference to thee whether thou art cold or warm, if thou art doing thy duty; and whether thou art drowsy or satisfied with sleep; and whether ill-spoken of or praised; and whether dying or doing something else." -**Marcus Aurelius**

"The warrior doesn't care if he's called a beast or a dog; the main thing is winning."
-**Hoobie Asakura Norikage**

"Mental bearing (calmness), not skill, is the sign of a matured samurai. A Samurai therefore should neither be pompous nor arrogant." -**Tsukahara Bokuden**

"Discipline is the soul of an army. It makes small numbers formidable; procures success to the weak, and esteem to all." -**George Washington**

"To be capable of fancies and imaginations, is common to man and beast. To be violently drawn and moved by the lusts and desires of the soul, is proper to wild beasts and monsters, such as Phalaris and Nero were." -**Marcus Aurelius**

"Without doubt, ferocious and disordered men are much weaker than timid and ordered ones. For order chases fear from men and disorder lessens ferocity." -**Machiavelli**

"Your army is resplendent with purple and gold. No one who had not seen it could conceive of its magnificence; but it will not be of any avail against the terrible energy of the Greeks. Their minds are bent on something very different from idle show. They are intent on securing the substantial excellence of their weapons, and on acquiring the discipline and the hardihood essential for the most efficient use of them. They will despise all your parade of purple and gold. They will not even value it as plunder. They glory in their ability to dispense with all the luxuries and conveniences of life. They live upon the coarsest food. At night they sleep upon the bare ground. By day they are always on the march. They brave hunger, cold, and every species of exposure with pride and pleasure, having the greatest contempt for any thing like softness and effeminacy of character. All this pomp and pageantry, with inefficient weapons, and inefficient men to wield them, will be of no avail against their invincible courage and energy; and the best disposition that you can make of all your gold, and silver, and other treasures, is to send it away and procure good soldiers with it." -**Charidemus to King Darius of Persia.**

"Given, then, that your troopers are thoroughly trained..., it is necessary, I presume, that they should further be instructed in a type of evolution the effect of which will show itself... in the manouvres of the exercising-ground; in the valorous onslaught of real battle when occasion calls; and in the ease with which whole regiments will prosecute their march, or cross a river, or thread a defile without the slightest symptom of confusion." -**Xenophon**

"The undisturbed mind is like the calm body water reflecting the brilliance of the moon. Empty the mind and you will realize the undisturbed mind." -**Yagyu Jubei**

"The mind which is free from passions is a citadel." -**Marcus Aurelius**

"Be like the promontory against which the waves continually break, but it stands firm and tames the fury of the water around it." -**Marcus Aurelius**

"It may be perhaps be thought a little irksome to be perpetually marching out, when there is no war; but all the same, I would have you call your men together and impress upon them the need to train themselves." -**Xenophon**

"It stands to reason, however, that in order to be able to inflict real damage upon a greatly superior force, the weaker combatant must possess such a moral superiority over the other as shall enable him to appear in the position of an expert, trained in all the feats of cavalry performance in the field, and leave his enemy to play the part of raw recruits or amateurs." -**Xenophon**

"I want to succeed in the thing I started out to do. I hate failure. I hate quitters."
-**Audie Murphy**

"When thou hast been compelled by circumstances to be disturbed in a manner, quickly return to thyself, and do not continue out of tune longer than the compulsion lasts; for thou wilt have more mastery over the harmony by continually recurring to it."
-**Marcus Aurelius**

"I cannot consent to place in the control of others one who cannot control himself."
-**Robert E. Lee**

"Discipline can only be obtained when all officers are so imbued with the sense of their awful obligation to their men and to their country that they cannot tolerate negligence. Officers who fail to correct errors or to praise excellence are valueless in peace and dangerous misfits in war." -**General Patton**

"All our writers agree that never more than two legions, besides auxiliaries, were sent under the command of each consul against the most numerous armies of the enemies. Such was the dependence on their discipline and resolution that this number was thought sufficient for any war they were engaged in." **-Publius Flavius Vegetius Renatus**

"I like whiskey. I always did, and that is why I never drink it." **-Robert E. Lee**

"If a thing is difficult to be accomplished by thyself, do not think that it is impossible for man: but if anything is possible for man and conformable to his nature, think that this can be attained by thyself too." **-Marcus Aurelius**

"But reverse the picture. Suppose men and horses to have been taught and trained to leap trenches and scale dykes, to spring up banks, and plunge from heights without scathe, to gallop headlong at full speed adown a steep: they will tower over unpractised opponents as the birds of the air tower over creatures that crawl and walk. Their feet are case-hardened by constant training, and, when it comes to tramping over rough ground, must differ from the uninitiated as the sound man from the lame. And so again, when it comes to charging and retiring, the onward-dashing gallop, the well-skilled, timely retreat, expert knowledge of the ground and scenery will assert superiority over inexpertness like that of eyesight over blindness." **-Xenophon**

"The gentleman does not needlessly and unnecessarily remind an offender of a wrong he may have committed against him. He can not only forgive; he can forget; and he strives for that nobleness of self and mildness of character which imparts sufficient strength to let the past be put the past." **-Robert E. Lee**

"No joining others in their wailing, no violent emotion." **-Marcus Aurelius**

"No ruler should put troops into the field merely to gratify his own spleen; no general should fight a battle simply out of pique." -**Sun Tzu**

"In the gymnastic exercises, suppose that a man has torn thee with his nails, and by dashing against thy head has inflicted a wound. Well, we neither show any signs of vexation, nor are we offended, nor do we suspect him afterwards as a treacherous fellow; and yet we are on our guard against him, not however as an enemy, nor yet with suspicion, but we quietly get out of his way. Something like this let thy behavior be in all the other parts of life; let us overlook many things in those who are like antagonists in the gymnasium. For it is in our power, as I said, to get out of the way, and to have no suspicion nor hatred." -**Marcus Aurelius**

"Americans never quit." -**Douglas MacArthur**

"For reason will convince us that what is necessary to be performed in the heat of action should constantly be practiced in the leisure of peace."
-**Publius Flavius Vegetius Renatus**

"Meddle not with many things, if thou wilt live cheerfully. Certainly there is nothing better, than for a man to confine himself to necessary actions." -**Marcus Aurelius**

"You can have anything you want – if you want it badly enough. You can be anything you want to be, have anything you desire, accomplish anything you set out to accomplish - if you will hold to that desire with singleness of purpose." -**Robert E. Lee**

"If you see the President, tell him from me that whatever happens there will be no turning back." -**Ulysses S. Grant**

"I do my duty: other things trouble me not; for they are either things without life, or things without reason, or things that have rambled and know not the way."
**-Marcus Aurelius**

"I will guard my ways, lest I sin with my tongue; I will restrain my mouth with a muzzle when the wicked are before me." **-King David**

"In the morning when thou risest unwillingly, let this thought be present: I am rising to the work of a human being. Why then am I dissatisfied if I am going to do the things for which I exist and for which I was brought into the world? Or have I been made for this, to lie in the bed-clothes and keep myself warm?" **-Marcus Aurelius**

"Occupy thyself with few things, says the philosopher, if thou wouldst be tranquil."
**-Marcus Aurelius**

"One of the primary purposes of discipline is to produce alertness. A man who is so lethargic that he fails to salute will fall an easy victim to the enemy." **-General Patton**

"Age wrinkles the body. Quitting wrinkles the soul." **-Douglas MacArthur**

"We shall defend our island, whatever the cost may be, we shall fight on the beaches, we shall fight on the landing grounds, we shall fight in the fields and in the streets, we shall fight in the hills; we shall never surrender." **-Winston Churchill**

"Let the part of thy soul which leads and governs be undisturbed by the movements in the flesh, whether of pleasure or of pain; and let it not unite with them, but let it circumscribe itself and limit those effects to their parts." **-Marcus Aurelius**

"As the severity of military operations increases, so also must the sternness of the discipline. The zeal of the soldiers, their warlike instincts, and the interests and excitements of war may ensure obedience of orders and the cheerful endurance of perils and hardships during a short and prosperous campaign. But when fortune is dubious or adverse; when retreats as well as advances are necessary; when supplies fail, arrangements miscarry, and disasters impend, and when the struggle is protracted, men can only be persuaded to accept evil things by the lively realization of the fact that greater terrors await their refusal." -**Winston Churchill**

"Length of service or age alone will never form a military man, for after serving many years an undisciplined soldier is still a novice in his profession. Not only those under the masters at arms, but all the soldiers in general, were formerly trained incessantly in those drills ... By practice only can be acquired agility of body and the skill requisite to engage an enemy with advantage, especially in close fight. But the most essential point of all is to teach soldiers to keep their ranks and never abandon their colors in the most difficult evolutions. Men thus trained are never at a loss amidst the greatest confusion of numbers." -**Publius Flavius Vegetius Renatus**

"Adorn thyself with simplicity and modesty." -**Marcus Aurelius**

"It's a difficult thing to truly know your own limits and points of weakness." -**Hagakure**

"Nature has fixed bounds... to eating and drinking, and yet thou goest beyond these bounds, beyond what is sufficient... So thou lovest not thyself, for if thou didst, thou wouldst love thy nature and her will." -**Marcus Aurelius**

"If, however, any man by using force stands in thy way, betake thyself to contentment and tranquillity, and at the same time employ the hindrance towards the exercise of some other virtue." -**Marcus Aurelius**

"In war discipline is superior to strength." -**Publius Flavius Vegetius Renatus**

"If while one part of your army is victorious the other should be defeated, you are by no means to despair, since even in this extremity the constancy and resolution of a general may recover a complete victory. There are innumerable instances where the party that gave least way to despair was esteemed the conqueror. For where losses and advantages seem nearly equal, he is reputed to have the superiority who bears up against his misfortunes with greatest resolution. He is therefore to be first, if possible, to seize the spoils of the slain and to make rejoicings for the victory. Such marks of confidence dispirit the enemy and redouble your own courage." -**Publius Flavius Vegetius Renatus**

"In a word, thy life is short. Thou must turn to profit the present by the aid of reason and justice. Be sober in thy relaxation." -**Marcus Aurelius**

"Disciplined and calm, to await the appearance of disorder and hubbub amongst the enemy: this is the art of retaining self-possession." -**Sun Tzu**

"It is not right to vex ourselves at things, for they care nought about it."
-**Marcus Aurelius**

"Victory belongs to the most persevering." -**Napoleon Bonaparte**

"Go forward until the last round is fired and the last drop of gas is expended...then go forward on foot!" -**General Patton**

"It is a shame for the soul to be first to give way in this life, when thy body does not give way." -**Marcus Aurelius**

"If you are going to win any battle, you have to do one thing. You have to make the mind run the body. Never let the body tell the mind what to do... the body is never tired if the mind is not tired." -**General Patton**

"If in training soldiers commands are habitually enforced, the army will be well-disciplined; if not, its discipline will be bad." -**Sun Tzu**

"It is thy duty to leave another man's wrongful act there where it is." -**Marcus Aurelius**

"You're never beaten until you admit it." -**General Patton**

"It is thy duty to order thy life well in every single act; and if every act does its duty as far as is possible, be content; and no one is able to hinder thee so that each act shall not do its duty." -**Marcus Aurelius**

"Pressure makes diamonds." -**General Patton**

"Do not disturb thyself by thinking of the whole of thy life. Let not thy thoughts at once embrace all the various troubles which thou mayest expect to befall thee: but on every occasion ask thyself, What is there in this which is intolerable and past bearing?" -**Marcus Aurelius**

"Success is how high you bounce when you hit bottom." -**General Patton**

"You cannot be disciplined in great things and undisciplined in small things. Brave undisciplined men have no chance against the discipline and valour of other men. Have you ever seen a few policemen handle a crowd?" -**General Patton**

"I don't fear failure. I only fear the slowing up of the engine inside of me which is saying, "Keep going, someone must be on top, why not you?" -**General Patton**

"The merit of an action lies in finishing it to the end." -**Genghis Khan**

"Don't give up the ship!" -**Last words of Captain James Lawrence.**

"The pain which is intolerable carries us off; but that which lasts a long time is tolerable; and the mind maintains its own tranquility by retiring into itself, and the ruling faculty is not made worse." -**Marcus Aurelius**

"Mental bearing (calmness), not skill, is the sign of a matured samurai. A Samurai therefore should neither be pompous nor arrogant." -**Tsukahara Bokuden**

"In the constitution of the rational animal, I see no virtue which is opposed to justice; but I see a virtue which is opposed to love of pleasure, and that is temperance."
-**Marcus Aurelius**

"Discipline is the soul of an army. It makes small numbers formidable, procures success to the weak, and esteem to all." -**George Washington**

"It is no good saying 'We are doing our best.' We have got to succeed in doing what it necessary." -**Winston Churchill**

"I do the very best I know how – the very best I can; and I mean to keep doing it until the end." -**Abraham Lincoln**

"Never give in! Never give in! Never, never, never – in nothing great or small, large or petty – never give in except to convictions of honor and good sense."
**-Winston Churchill**


"Victory at all costs, victory in spite of terror, victory no matter how long and hard the road may be; for without victory, there is no survival." **-Winston Churchill**


"Every position must be held to the last man: there must be no retirement. With our backs to the wall, and believing in the justice of our cause, each one of us must fight on to the end." **-Lord Haig**


"[The Spartans] are free – yes – but not entirely free; for they have a master, and that master is Law, which they fear much more than your subjects fear you. Whatever this master commands, they do; and his command never varies: it is never to retreat in battle, however great the odds, but always to stand firm, and to conquer or die." **-Demaratus**


"If you dislike the idea of a subordinate position, stay keep out of the war altogether."
**-Ancient Spartan officer Syagrus.**


"I am a Roman. I came here to kill you, my enemy. It is the Roman way to do and suffer bravely." **-Gaius Mucius Scaevola**


"The strong manly ones in life are those who understand the meaning of the word patience. Patience means restraining one's inclinations. There are seven emotions: joy, anger, anxiety, adoration, grief, fear, and hate, and if a man does not give way to these he can be called patient. I am not as strong as I might be, but I have long known and practiced patience. And if my descendants wish to be as I am, they must study patience."
**-Tokugawa Ieyasu**

"The sentry who is inattentive will be killed.  The arrow-messenger who gets drunk will be killed… the warrior who unlawfully appropriates booty for himself will be killed. The leader who is incompetent will be killed." **-Laws of Genghis Khan**

"There must be a beginning of any great matter, but the continuing unto the end until it be thoroughly finished yields the true glory." **-Sir Francis Drake**

"It is of much more importance that a soldier should be strong than tall."
**-Publius Flavius Vegetius Renatus**

"No state can either be happy or secure that is remiss and negligent in the discipline of its troops. For it is not profusion of riches or excess of luxury that can influence our enemies to court or respect us." **-Publius Flavius Vegetius Renatus**

"Of all the sentiments that enslave our heart, none could be more disastrous for those which feel the impulse, one most contrary to one's humanity and which carries the risk of one becoming hostile to the entire world, than an ambition put out of order, than an aching desire for glory.  A private individual who has the misfortune to have been born with this lust for power is more miserable than mad.  He is dulled to the present, and exists only in the future or in imaginary times; nothing in the world can satisfy him, and the drunken ambition which has mastered him always adulterates the softness of his pleasures with bitterness.  An ambitious prince is more unhappy than a private individual; because his madness, being proportioned to his position, is vaguer, more disobedient and more unstable." **-Frederick the Great**

"Let me alone: I have yet my legs and one arm. Tell the surgeon to make haste and his instruments. I know I must lose my right arm, so the sooner it's off the better." **-Horatio Nelson, after being wounded during the attack on Santa Cruz de Tenerife (July 24. 1797).**

"The man who will go where his colors go without asking, who will fight a phantom foe in a jungle or a mountain range, and who will suffer and die; in the midst of incredible hardship, without complaint, is still what he has always been, from Imperial Rome to sceptered Britain to democratic America. He is the stuff of which legends are made. His pride is his colors and his regiment, his training hard and thorough and coldly realistic, to fit him for what he must face, and his obedience is to his orders. As a legionnaire, he held the gates of civilization for the classical world...today he is called United States Marine." **-Lt. Col Fehrenbach**

"England expects that every man will do his duty." **-Horatio Nelson, signal to the British fleet before the Battle of Trafalgar.**

"Weakness is a step towards danger and depravity is a sign of doom."
**-Huang Shi Gong**

"These are the times that try men's souls. The summer soldier and the sunshine patriot will, in this crisis, shrink from the service of their country; but he that stands it now deserves the love and thanks of man and woman. Tyranny, like hell, is not easily conquered; yet we have this consolation with us, that the harder the conflict, the more glorious the triumph." **-Tom Paine, in an address read to the American soldiers during the struggle for independence before they crossed the Delaware to launch an offensive.**

"Be prepared in mind by having disciplined yourself to be obedient to every order, and also by having thought out before hand any accident or situation that might occur, so that you know the right thing to do at the right moment, and are willing to do it. Be prepared in body by making yourself strong and active and able to do the right thing at the right moment, and do it." **-Robert Baden-Powell**

"A scout in the army, as you know, is generally a soldier who is chosen for his cleverness and pluck... They understand how to live out in the jungle. They can find their way anywhere, and are able to read meanings from the smallest signs and foot tracks. They know how to look after their health when they are far away from doctors. They are strong and plucky, ready to face danger, and always keen to help each other. They are accustomed to take their lives in their hands, and to risk them without hesitation if they can help their country by doing so. They give up everything, their personal comforts and desires, in order to get their work done. They do it because it is their duty." -**Robert Baden-Powell**

"It is not courage but it is weakness to be unable to endure a short period of privation. It is easier to find men who will voluntarily risk death than men who will bear suffering patiently." -**Julius Caesar, reporting the words of the Gaulish leader Critognatus.**

"One who indulges himself while instructing others is contrary to the natural order." -**Huang Shi Gong**

"One who is able to hold what he possesses will feel secure; one who is greedy for what others have will be asking for disaster." -**Huang Shi Gong**

"No man is to be employed in the field who is not trained and tested in discipline." -**Publius Flavius Vegetius Renatus**

"A Scout saying is 'never say die till you're dead' – and if he acts up to this, it will pull him out of many a bad place when everything seems to be going wrong for him. It means a mixture of pluck, patience and strength, which we call endurance." -**Robert Baden-Powell**

"A large number of the best sportsmen, soldiers, sailors and others, do not smoke – they find they can do better without it. No boy ever began smoking because he liked it, but generally because he either feared being chaffed by the other boys or because he thought that by smoking he would look like a great man – when all the time, he only looks like a little ass." **-Robert Baden-Powell**

"Victory in war does not depend entirely upon numbers or mere courage; only skill and discipline will insure it. We find that the Romans owed the conquest of the world to no other cause than continual military training, exact observance of discipline in their camps and unwearied cultivation of the other arts of war."
**-Publius Flavius Vegetius Renatus**

"A captain sticks to the ship till the last. Why? She is only a lump of iron and wood, and his life is as valuable as that of any of the women and children on board. But he makes everybody get away safely before he attempts to save his more valuable [compared to the ship's] life. Why? Because the ship is his ship, and he has been taught that it is duty to stick to it, and he considers it would be dishonorable in him to do otherwise – so he puts honor before safety." **-Robert Baden-Powell**

"Are you still to learn that the end and perfection of our victories is to avoid the vices and infirmities of those whom we subdue?" **-Alexander the Great**

"But it might be closer to the truth to assume that the faculty known as self-control - the gift of keeping calm even under the greatest stress - is rooted in temperament. It is itself an emotion which serves to balance the passionate feelings in strong characters without destroying them, and it is this balance alone that assures the dominance of the intellect..." **-Karl von Clausewitz**

"I propose to fight it out on this line, if it takes all summer." **-Ulysses S. Grant**

"The commander should practice kindness and severity, should appear friendly to the soldiers, speak to them on the march, visit them while they are cooking, ask them if they are well cared for, and alleviate their needs if they have any. Officers without experience in war should be treated kindly. Their good actions should be praised. Small requests should be granted and they should not be treated in an overbearing manner, but severity is maintained about everything regarding the service. The negligent officer is punished; the man who answers back is made to feel your severity by being reprimanded with the authoritative air that superiority gives; pillaging or argumentative soldiers, or those whose obedience is not immediate should be punished." -**Frederick the Great**


"In seeking to upset the enemy's balance, a commander must not lose his own balance. He needs to have the quality which Voltaire described as the keystone of Marlborough's success - 'that calm courage in the midst of tumult, that serenity of soul in danger, which the English call a cool head.' But to it he must add the quality for which the French have found the most aptly descriptive phrase - 'le sens du practicable'. The sense of what is possible, and what is not possible - tactically and administratively. The combination of both these two 'guarding' qualities might be epitomised as the power of cool calculation. The sands of history are littered with the wrecks of finely conceived plans that capsized for want of ballast." -**Captain Sir Basil Liddell Hart**


"Self-control is the chief element in self-respect, and self-respect is the chief element in courage." -**Thucydides**


"To be disciplined does not mean to keep silent, to do only what one thinks can be done without risk or being compromised, the art of avoiding responsibilities, but it means acting in the spirit of the orders received, and to that end assuring by thought and planning the possibility of carrying out such orders, assuring by strength of character the energy to assume the risks necessary in their execution. The laziness of the mind results in lack of discipline as much as does insubordination. Lack of ability and ignorance are not either excuses, for knowledge is within reach of all who seek it." -**Ferdinand Foch**

"Battles are decided in favor of the troops whose bravery, fortitude, and especially, whose endurance, surpasses that of the enemy's; the army with the higher breaking point wins the decision." **-George C. Marshall**

"The great thing about Grant, I take it, is his perfect coolness and persistency of purpose. I judge he is not easily excited - which is a great element in an officer -and he has the grit of a bulldog. Once let him get his 'teeth' in, and nothing can shake him loose." **-Abraham Lincoln**

"The merit of the action lies in finishing it to the end." **-Genghis Khan**

# Chapter 7
# Wisdom, Faith and Belief

*L*iving on the edge between life and death gives a unique perspective to the two great realities of life and death. Many warriors throughout the ages have sought a higher purpose in life – a sense that there's more to life than just what can be seen, and that there's something bigger than their own personal sensibilities. One of the best examples of this warrior ethic was the Roman Emperor Marcus Aurelius, who wrote his "Meditations" while on the front lines in Germany.

It is uncertain who first said that there are no atheists in foxholes, but many warriors facing danger have looked to a higher power to help them out of a dire situation, or for comfort that a valiant death will be rewarded after death. After a narrow escape from defeat or death, many a soldier has felt as if somebody or something needed to be thanked. This natural feeling was perhaps best expressed in what Oliver Cromwell didn't actually say but probably wished he had: "Trust in God, but keep your powder dry."

---

"God has given to man no sharper spur to victory than contempt of death." **-Hannibal**

"Be of one mind and one faith, that you may conquer your enemies and lead long and happy lives." **-Genghis Khan**

"Prohibit the taking of omens, and do away with superstitious doubts. Then, until death itself comes, no calamity need be feared." **-Sun Tzu**

"Intelligence is the flower of discrimination. There are many examples of the flower blooming but not bearing fruit." -**Nabeshima Naoshige**

"He is blind, who cannot see with the eyes of his understanding." -**Marcus Aurelius**

"Given enough time, any man may master the physical. With enough knowledge, any man may become wise. It is the true warrior who can master both....and surpass the result." -**Tien T'ai**

"Love the art, poor as it may be, which thou hast learned, and be content with it; and pass through the rest of life like one who has entrusted to the gods with his whole soul all that he has, making thyself neither the tyrant nor the slave of any man."
-**Marcus Aurelius**

"In life quality is what counts, not quantity." -**Audie Murphy**

"It is no evil for things to undergo change, and no good for things to subsist in consequence of change. Time is like a river made up of the events which happen, and a violent stream; for as soon as a thing has been seen, it is carried away, and another comes in its place, and this will be carried away too." -**Marcus Aurelius**

"If fear is cultivated it will become stronger; if faith is cultivated it will achieve mastery." -**Admiral John Paul Jones**

"Every moment think steadily as a Roman and a man to do what thou hast in hand with perfect and simple dignity, and feeling of affection, and freedom, and justice, and to give thyself relief from all other thoughts." -**Marcus Aurelius**

"Let correct views of life, and learn to see the world in its true light. It will enable you to live pleasantly, to do good, and, when summoned away, to leave without regret."
-**Robert E. Lee**

"If any god told thee that thou shalt die to-morrow, or certainly on the day after to-morrow, thou wouldst not care much whether it was on the third day or on the morrow, unless thou wast in the highest degree mean-spirited; for how small is the difference. So think it no great thing to die after as many years as thou canst name rather than to-morrow." -**Marcus Aurelius**

"Warfare which is invariably in accord with righteousness is the means by which to incite masses and be victorious over the enemy." -**Jiang Taigong**

"Truly I think he that prays and preaches best will fight best." -**Oliver Cromwell**

"The end and object of a rational constitution is, to do nothing rashly, to be kindly affected towards men, and in all things willingly to submit unto the gods."
-**Marcus Aurelius**

"In all my perplexities and distresses, the Bible has never failed to give me light and strength." -**Robert E. Lee**

"It is right to be content with that which happens to thee." -**Marcus Aurelius**

"How hast thou behaved hitherto to the gods, thy parents, brethren, children, teachers, to those who looked after thy infancy, to thy friends, kinsfolk, to thy slaves? Consider if thou hast hitherto behaved to all in such a way that this may be said of thee: 'Never has he wronged a man in deed or word." -**Marcus Aurelius**

"The education of a man is never completed until he dies." -**Robert E. Lee**

"Do not then consider life a thing of any value. For look to the immensity of time behind thee, and to the time which is before thee, another boundless space. In this infinity then what is the difference between him who lives three days and him who lives three generations?" -**Marcus Aurelius**

"Let your course by the stars, not by the lights of every passing ship." -**Omar Bradley**

"What art and profession soever thou hast learned, endeavour to affect it, and comfort thyself in it; and pass the remainder of thy life as one who from his whole heart commits himself and whatsoever belongs unto him, unto the gods: and as for men, carry not thyself either tyrannically or servilely towards any." -**Marcus Aurelius**

"I had rather excel others in the knowledge of what is excellent, than in the extent of my power and dominion." -**Alexander the Great.**

"Thou canst pass thy life in an equable flow of happiness, if thou canst go by the right way, and think and act in the right way." -**Marcus Aurelius**

"The Sage King does not take pleasure in using the army. He mobilizes it to execute the violently perverse and punish the rebellious. Using righteousness to execute unrighteous is like releasing the pent-up river to douse a torch, or pushing a person teetering at the edge of a cliff... War should only be a last resort, and only then it accords with Heaven." -**Huang Shi Gong**

"When I consider the heavens, the work of your fingers, the moon and the stars, which you have ordained, what is man that you are mindful of him, and the son of man that you visit him?" -**King David**

"This also thou must observe, that whatsoever it is that naturally doth happen to things natural, hath somewhat in itself that is pleasing and delightful: as a great loaf when it is baked, some parts of it cleave as it were, and part asunder, and make the crust of it rugged and unequal, and yet those parts of it, though in some sort it be against the art and intention of baking itself, that they are thus cleft and parted, which should have been and were first made all even and uniform, they become it well nevertheless, and have a certain peculiar property, to stir the appetite." -**Marcus Aurelius**

"Look within. Let neither the peculiar quality of anything nor its value escape thee."
-**Marcus Aurelius**

"If one's behavior does not accord with the Way and righteousness, but dwells in magnificence and enjoys power, disaster will inevitably befall him." -**Wu Qi**

"Be not disgusted, nor discouraged, nor dissatisfied, if thou dost not succeed in doing everything according to right principles, but when thou hast failed, return back again, and be content if the greater part of what thou dost is consistent with man's nature, and love this to which thou returnest." -**Marcus Aurelius**

"And thou wilt give thyself relief if thou dost every act of thy life as if it were the last."
-**Marcus Aurelius**

"Ever consider and think upon the world as being but one living substance, and having but one soul, and how all things in the world, are terminated into one sensitive power."
-**Marcus Aurelius**

"Life is a lively process of becoming." -**Douglas MacArthur**

"The Way, virtue, benevolence, righteousness and forms of propriety are one body. The Way are the common principles men follow. Virtue is what men understand and gains when they follow the Way. Benevolence is love and care among the humans. Righteousness is what people should do. Forms of propriety regulate the behavior of people. There cannot be lack of any one of them. Thus everyday our actions should be regulated by forms of propriety. Punishing brigands and taking revenge are decisions of righteousness. The compassionate heart is an expression of benevolence. To right oneself and gain the respect of others is the path of virtue. Ensuring that all people are equal and do not lose what they have gained, this is the work of the Way."
**-Huang Shi Gong**


"Such an enemy [one that is stronger and with the advantage of the terrain] cannot be overcome by force alone, but by the wisdom of the sage." **-Wu Qi**


"If thou shalt intend that which is present, following the rule of right and reason carefully, solidly, meekly, and shalt not intermix any other businesses, but shall study this only to preserve thy spirit unpolluted, and pure, and shall cleave unto him without either hope or fear of anything, in all things that thou shalt either do or speak, contenting thyself with heroical truth, thou shalt live happily; and from this, there is no man that can hinder thee." **-Marcus Aurelius**


"All under Heaven is not the domain of one person, but the domain for all those under Heaven. Anyone who shares profit with all the people under Heaven will gain the kingdom. Anyone who monopolize the profits will lose the kingdom. Heaven has its four seasons and the Earth, its resources. Being capable of sharing these with populace is truly benevolent. Whoever has true benevolence, all under Heaven will pledge allegiance to him." **-Jiang Taigong**


"Do nothing against thy will, nor contrary to the community, nor without due examination, nor with reluctancy. Affect not to set out thy thoughts with curious neat language. Be neither a great talker, nor a great undertaker." **-Marcus Aurelius**

"What then is worth being valued? To be received with clapping of hands? No. Neither must we value the clapping of tongues; for the praise which comes from the many is a clapping of tongues. Suppose then that thou hast given up this worthless thing called fame, what remains that is worth valuing? This, in my opinion: to move thyself and to restrain thyself in conformity to thy proper constitution, to which end both all employments and arts lead." -**Marcus Aurelius**

"Do not be afraid when one becomes rich, when the glory of his house is increased; for when he dies he shall carry nothing away." -**King David**

"Observe good faith and justice towards all nations; cultivate peace and harmony with all." -**George Washington**.

"But to reverence and honor thy own mind will make thee content with thyself, and in harmony with society, and in agreement with the gods, that is, praising all that they give and have ordered." -**Marcus Aurelius**

"People grow old only by deserting their ideals. Years may wrinkle the skin, but to give up interest wrinkles the soul. You are as young as your faith, as old as your doubt; as young as your self-confidence, as old as your fear; as young as your hope as old as your despair. In the central place of every heart, there is a recording chamber. So long as it receives messages of beauty, hope, cheer and courage, so long are you young. When your heart is covered with the snows of pessimism and the ice of cynicism, then, and then only, are you grown old. And then, indeed as the ballad says, you just fade away." -**Douglas MacArthur**

"For what is more agreeable than wisdom itself, when thou thinkest of the security and the happy course of all things which depend on the faculty of understanding and knowledge?" -**Marcus Aurelius**

"They attacked me at a moment when I was weakest, but the LORD upheld me. He led me to a place of safety; he rescued me because he delights in me. The LORD rewarded me for doing right; he compensated me because of my innocence. For I have kept the ways of the LORD; I have not turned from my God to follow evil. For all his laws are constantly before me; I have never abandoned his principles. I am blameless before God; I have kept myself from sin. The LORD rewarded me for doing right, because of the innocence of my hands in his sight." **-King David**

"The universal nature out of the universal substance, as if it were wax, now moulds a horse, and when it has broken this up, it uses the material for a tree, then for a man, then for something else; and each of these things subsists for a very short time. But it is no hardship for the vessel to be broken up, just as there was none in its being fastened together." **-Marcus Aurelius**

"A general must know the ways of heaven, the advantages of terrain and human affairs." **-Jiang Taigong**

"Since it is possible that thou mayest depart from life this very moment, regulate every act and thought accordingly." **-Marcus Aurelius**

"For it is not lawful, that anything that is of another and inferior kind and nature, be it what it will, as either popular applause, or honour, or riches, or pleasures; should be suffered to confront and contest as it were, with that which is rational, and operatively good." **-Marcus Aurelius**

"Towards human beings, as they have reason, behave in a social spirit. And on all occasions call on the gods." **-Marcus Aurelius**

"I believe that forgiving them is God's function. Our job is to arrange the meeting." **-General Norman Schwarzkopf**

"Unorthodox and orthodox tactics are produced from inexhaustible resources of the mind." -**Jiang Taigong**

"Nothing happens to any man which he is not formed by nature to bear."
-**Marcus Aurelius**

"But death certainly, and life... pain and pleasure – all these things equally happen to good men and bad, being things which make us neither better nor worse. Therefore they are neither good nor evil." -**Marcus Aurelius**

"The end and aim of the Cynic philosophy, as indeed of every philosophy, is happiness, but happiness that consists in living according to nature, and not according to the opinions of the multitude." -**Flavius Claudius Julianus**

"One thing only troubles me, lest I should do something which the constitution of man does not allow, or in the way which it does not allow, or what it does not allow now."
-**Marcus Aurelius**

"Often think of the rapidity with which things pass by and disappear, both the things which are and the things which are produced. For substance is like a river in a continual flow, and the activities of things are in constant change, and the causes work in infinite varieties; and there is hardly anything which stands still. And consider this which is near to thee, this boundless abyss of the past and of the future in which all things disappear. How then is he not a fool who is puffed up with such things or plagued about them and makes himself miserable? For they vex him only for a time, and a short time."
-**Marcus Aurelius**

"How quickly all things disappear – in the universe, the bodies themselves, but in time, the remembrance of them." -**Marcus Aurelius**

"Think not so much of what thou hast not as of what thou hast: but of the things which thou hast select the best, and then reflect how eagerly they would have been sought, if thou hadst them not. At the same time, however, take care that thou dost not through being so pleased with them accustom thyself to overvalue them, so as to be disturbed if ever thou shouldst not have them." -**Marcus Aurelius**

"God arms me with strength; he has made my way safe. He makes me as surefooted as a deer, leading me safely along the mountain heights. He prepares me for battle; he strengthens me to draw a bow of bronze. You have given me the shield of your salvation. Your right hand supports me; your gentleness has made me great. You have made a wide path for my feet to keep them from slipping. I chased my enemies and caught them; I did not stop until they were conquered. I struck them down so they could not get up; they fell beneath my feet. You have armed me with strength for the battle; you have subdued my enemies under my feet. You made them turn and run; I have destroyed all who hated me... I ground them as fine as dust carried by the wind. I swept them into the gutter like dirt. You gave me victory over my accusers. You appointed me as the ruler over nations; people I don't even know now serve me." -**King David**

"Reverence that which is best in the universe; and this is that which makes use of all things and directs all things. And in like manner also reverence that which is best in thyself." -**Marcus Aurelius**

"Though thou shouldest be going to live three thousand years, and as many times ten thousand years, still remember that no man loses any other life than this which he now lives, nor lives any other than this which he now loses. The longest and shortest are thus brought to the same." -**Marcus Aurelius**

"Through God we will do valiantly, for it is He who shall tread down our enemies." -**King David**

"We ought to observe also that even the things which follow after the things which are produced according to nature contain something pleasing and attractive. For instance, when bread is baked some parts are split at the surface, and these parts which thus open, and have a certain fashion contrary to the purpose of the baker's art, are beautiful in a manner, and in a peculiar way excite a desire for eating. And again, figs, when they are quite ripe, gape open; and in the ripe olives the very circumstance of their being near to rottenness adds a peculiar beauty to the fruit. And the ears of corn bending down, and the lion's eyebrows, and the foam which flows from the mouth of wild boars, and many other things – though they are far from being beautiful if a man should examine them severally – still, because they are consequent upon the things which are formed by nature, help to adorn them, and they please the mind; so that if a man should have a feeling and deeper insight with respect to the things which are produced in the universe, there is hardly one of those which follow by way of consequence which will not seem to him to be in a manner disposed so as to give pleasure. And so he will see even the real gaping jaws of wild beasts with no less pleasure than those which painters and sculptors show by imitation; and in an old woman and an old man he will be able to see a certain maturity and comeliness; and the attractive loveliness of young persons he will be able to look on with chaste eyes; and many such things will present themselves, not pleasing to every man, but to him only who has become truly familiar with Nature and her works." -**Marcus Aurelius**

"There are but two powers in the world, the sword and the mind. In the long run the sword is always beaten by the mind." -**Napoleon Bonaparte**

"As our enemies have found, we can reason like men, so now let us show them we can fight like men also." -**Thomas Jefferson**

"Know thy self, know thy enemy. A thousand battles, a thousand victories." -**Sun Tzu**

"Labor not unwillingly, nor without regard to the common interest, nor without due consideration, nor with distraction; nor let studied ornament set off thy thoughts, and be not either a man of many words, or busy about too many things." -**Marcus Aurelius**

"If the impulse to daring and bravery is too fierce and violent, stay it with guidance and instruction." -**Xun Zi**

"Throwing away then all things, hold to these only which are few; and besides, bear in mind that every man lives only this present time, which is an indivisible point, and that all the rest of his life is either past or it is uncertain. Short then is the time which every man lives, and small the nook of the earth where he lives; and short too the longest posthumous fame." -**Marcus Aurelius**

"We shrink from change; yet is there anything that can come into being without it? What does Nature hold dearer, or more proper to herself? Could you have a hot bath unless the firewood underwent some change? ...Is it possible for any useful thing to be achieved without change? Do you not see, then, that change in yourself is of the same order and no less necessary to Nature?" -**Marcus Aurelius**

"Let not future things disturb thee, for thou wilt come to them, if it shall be necessary, having with thee the same reason which now thou usest for present things."
-**Marcus Aurelius**

"The more I study the world, the more I am convinced of the inability of brute force to create anything durable." -**Napoleon**

"Remember that very little is needed to make a happy life." -**Marcus Aurelius**

"Keep in mind how many things you yourself have already seen change. The universe is change. Life is understanding." -**Marcus Aurelius**

"True genius resides in the capacity for evaluation of uncertain, hazardous and conflicting information." -**Winston Churchill**

"All men dream, but not equally. Those who dream by night in the dusty recesses of their minds wake in the day to find that it was vanity: but the dreamers of the day are dangerous men, for they may act their dream with open eyes, to make it possible."
-**Lawrence of Arabia**

"That which is not good for the swarm, neither is it good for the bee."
-**Marcus Aurelius**

"We make a living by what we get, but we make a life by what we give."
-**Winston Churchill**

"You haven't learnt life's lesson very well if you haven't noticed that you can give the tone or color, or decide the reaction you want of people in advance. It's unbelievably simple. If you want them to take an interest in you, take an interest in them first. If you want to make them nervous, become nervous yourself. If you want them to shout and raise their voices, raise yours and shout. If you want them to strike you, strike first. It's as simple as that. People will treat you as you treat them. It's no secret. Look about you. You can prove it with the next person you meet." -**Winston Churchill**

"There are two kinds of success. One is the very rare kind that comes to the man who has the power to do what no one else has the power to do. That is genius. But the average man who wins is not a genius. He is a man who has merely the ordinary qualities that he shares with his fellows, but who has developed those ordinary qualities to a more than ordinary degree." -**Theodore Roosevelt**

"The study of literature and the practice of the military arts must be pursued side by side." -**Tokugawa Ieyasu**

"Accustom thyself to attend carefully to what is said by another, and as much as it is possible, be in the speaker's mind." -**Marcus Aurelius**

"I am the flail of God. Had you not created great sins, God would not have sent a punishment like me upon you." -**Genghis Khan**

"If thou workest at that which is before thee, following right reason seriously, vigorously, calmly, without allowing anything else to distract thee, but keeping thy divine part pure, as if thou shouldst be bound to give it back immediately; if thou holdest to this, expecting nothing, fearing nothing, but satisfied with thy present activity according to nature, and with heroic truth in every word and sound which thou utterest, thou wilt live happy. And there is no man who is able to prevent this."
-**Marcus Aurelius**

"Life is like unto a long journey with a heavy burden. Let thy step be slow and steady, that thou stumble not. Persuade thyself that imperfection and inconvenience are the natural lot of mortals, and there will be no room for discontent, neither for despair. When ambitious desires arise in thy heart, recall the days of extremity thou has past through. Forbearance is the root of quietness and assurance forever. Look upon the wrath of the enemy. If thou knowest only what it is to conquer, and knowest not what it is like to be defeated, woe unto thee; it will fare ill with thee. Find fault with thyself rather than with others." -**Tokugawa Ieyasu**

"Within ten days thou wilt seem a god to those to whom thou art now a beast and an ape, if thou wilt return to thy principles and the worship of reason." -**Marcus Aurelius**

"It is better for a man to avenge his friend than to mourn him long.  We must all expect an end to life in this world; let him who can win fame before death, because that is a dead man's best memorial." -**Beowulf**

"Begin the morning by saying to thyself, I shall meet with the busybody, the ungrateful, arrogant, deceitful, envious, unsocial." -**Marcus Aurelius**

"The right hand of God gave me courage.  The right hand of God raised me up." -**Motto engraved on the sword of Roger I of Sicily.**

"Hast thou reason?...Why then dost not thou use it? For if this does its own work, what else dost thou wish?" -**Marcus Aurelius**

"Oh Lord!  Thou knowest how busy I must be this day; if I forget thee, do not thou forget me."  -**Pre-battle prayer of Sir Jacob Astley.**

"He who has seen present things has seen all, both everything which has taken place from all eternity and everything which will be for time without end; for all things are of one kin and of one form." -**Marcus Aurelius**

"We humans are foolish in many ways: we want to conquer all as if we had all time, as if our lives did not have any end.  Thus our real time passes too quickly, and often when one believes that they are working only for themselves, they are in fact working for unworthy or ungrateful successors."  -**Frederick the Great**

"Let no act be done without a purpose, nor otherwise than according to the perfect principles of art." -**Marcus Aurelius**

"Captain, my religious belief teaches me to feel as safe in battle as in bed. God has fixed the time for my death." **-Stonewall Jackson**

"If thou workest at that which is before thee, following right reason seriously, vigorously, calmly, without allowing anything else to distract thee, but keeping thy divine part pure, as if thou shouldst be bound to give it back immediately; if thou holdest to this, expecting nothing, fearing nothing, but satisfied with thy present activity according to nature, and with heroic truth in every word and sound which thou utterest, thou wilt live happy." **-Marcus Aurelius**

"It is no hard matter for many to be shut up in the hands of a few; and with the God of heaven it is all one, to deliver with a great multitude, or a small company: For the victory of battle standeth not in the multitude of an host; but strength cometh from heaven. They come against us in much pride and iniquity to destroy us, and our wives and children, and to spoil us: But we fight for our lives and our laws. Wherefore the Lord himself will overthrow them before our face: and as for you, be ye not afraid of them." **-Judas Maccabeus**

"Do not have such an opinion of things as he has who does thee wrong, or such as he wishes thee to have, but look at them as they are in truth." **-Marcus Aurelius**

"No man is much good unless he believes in God and obeys his Laws. So every Scout should have a religion." **-Robert Baden-Powell**

"Hast thou reason? I have. Why then makest thou not use of it? For if thy reason do her part, what more canst thou require?" **-Marcus Aurelius**

"While you are living your life on this earth, try to do something good which may remain after you." **-Robert Baden-Powell**

"Above all, do not distract or strain thyself, but be free, and look at things as a man, as a human being, as a citizen, as a mortal." -**Marcus Aurelius**

"With regard to these devices and to any others which invention may suggest towards capturing the foeman by force or fraud, I have one common word of advice to add, which is, to act with God, and then while Heaven propitious smiles, fortune will scarcely dare to frown." -**Xenophon**

"Remember that to change thy opinion and to follow him who corrects thy error is as consistent with freedom as it is to persist in thy error." -**Marcus Aurelius**

"Consider thyself to be dead, and to have completed thy life up to the present time; and live according to nature the remainder which is allowed thee. Love that only which happens to thee and is spun with the thread of thy destiny. For what is more suitable?" -**Marcus Aurelius**

"This is the chief thing: Be not perturbed, for all things are according to the nature of the universal; and in a little time thou wilt be nobody and nowhere...In the next place, having fixed thy eyes steadily on thy business look at it, and at the same time remembering that it is thy duty to be a good man, and what man's nature demands, do that without turning aside; and speak as it seems to thee most just, only let it be with a good disposition and with modesty and without hypocrisy." -**Marcus Aurelius**

"It is in thy power to live free from all compulsion in the greatest tranquillity of mind, even if all the world cry out against thee as much as they choose, and even if wild beasts tear in pieces the members of this kneaded matter which has grown around thee." -**Marcus Aurelius**

"The LORD is my shepherd; I shall not want.

He maketh me to lie down in green pastures: he leadeth me beside the still waters.

He restoreth my soul: he leadeth me in the paths of righteousness for his name's sake.

Yea, though I walk through the valley of the shadow of death, I will fear no evil: for thou art with me; thy rod and thy staff they comfort me.

Thou preparest a table before me in the presence of mine enemies: thou anointest my head with oil; my cup runneth over.

Surely goodness and mercy shall follow me all the days of my life: and I will dwell in the house of the LORD for ever." **-King David, Psalm 23**


"One thing have I desired of the LORD, that will I seek after; that I may dwell in the house of the LORD all the days of my life, to behold the beauty of the LORD, and to enquire in his temple. For in the time of trouble he shall hide me in his pavilion: in the secret of his tabernacle shall he hide me; he shall set me up upon a rock. And now shall mine head be lifted up above mine enemies round about me: therefore will I offer in his tabernacle sacrifices of joy; I will sing, yea, I will sing praises unto the LORD."
**-King David**


"Everything exists for some end,--a horse, a vine. Why dost thou wonder? Even the sun will say, I am for some purpose, and the rest of the gods will say the same. For what purpose then art thou – to enjoy pleasure? See if common sense allows this."
**-Marcus Aurelius**


"Short lived are both the praiser and the praised, and the rememberer and the remembered." **-Marcus Aurelius**


"If thou canst see sharp, look and judge wisely." **-Marcus Aurelius**


"The LORD is a man of war: The LORD is his name." **-Exodus 15:3**

"And now if the repetition of the phrase throughout this treatise "act with God," surprises any one, he may take my word for it that with the daily or hourly occurrence of perils which must betide him, his wonderment will diminish; as also with the clearer recognition of the fact that in time of war the antagonists are full of designs against each other, but the precise issue of these plots and counterplots is rarely known. To what counsellor, then, can a man apply for advice in his extremity save only to the gods, who know all things and forewarn whomsoever they will by victims or by omens, by voice or vision? Is it not rational to suppose that they will prefer to help in their need, not those who only seek them in time of momentary stress and trouble, but those rather who in the halcyon days of their prosperity make a practice of rendering to Heaven the service of heart and soul?" **-Xenophon**

"A chaplain visits our company. In a tired voice, he prays for the strength of our arms and for the souls of the men who are to die. We do not consider his denomination. Helmets come off. Catholics, Jews, and Protestants bow their heads and finger their weapons. It is the front-line religion: God and the Garand." **-Audie Murphy**

"Blessed are ye, who have fought like those at Bedr, who have been steadfast as Abu-Bekr, victorious as Omar, who have recalled the hosts of Othman and the onslaughts of Ali! Ye have renewed for Islam the glorious memories of Kadisiya, of the Yarmuk, of Khaibar, and of Khalid, the Sword of God. The Almighty recompense you, and accept the offering of the blood ye have shed in his service, and grant you Paradise, happy for ever." **-Prayer of Saladin**

"In forty hours I shall be in battle, with little information, and on the spur of the moment will have to make the most momentous decisions. But I believe that one's spirit enlarges with responsibility and that, with God's help, I shall make them and make them right." **-General Patton**

"Military power wins battles, but spiritual power wins wars." **-George Marshall**

"I pray daily to do my duty, retain my self-confidence, and accomplish my destiny. No one can live under the awful responsibility I have without Divine help. Frequently I feel that I don't rate it." -**General Patton**

"Captain, my religious belief teaches me to feel as safe in battle as in bed. God has fixed the time for my death. I do not concern myself about that, but to be always ready, no matter when it may overtake me... That is the way all men should live, and then all would be equally brave." -**Stonewall Jackson**

"I will smash them, so help me god!" -**Andrew Jackson**

"O Lord God, when Thou givest to thy servants to endeavour any great matter, grant us also to know that it is not the beginning, but the continuing of the same until it is thoroughly finished which yieldeth the true glory." -**Sir Francis Drake**

"He who fears death either fears the loss of sensation or a different kind of sensation. But if thou shalt have no sensation, neither wilt thou feel any harm; and if thou shalt acquire another kind of sensation, thou wilt be a different kind of living being and thou wilt not cease to live." -**Marcus Aurelius**

"He who does wrong does wrong against himself. He who acts unjustly acts unjustly to himself, because he makes himself bad." -**Marcus Aurelius**

"All of us, without being taught, have attained to a belief in some sort of divinity, though it is not easy for all men to know the precise truth about it, nor is it possible for those who do know it to tell it to all men." -**Flavius Claudius Julianus**

"I feel that my destiny is in the hands of the Almighty. This belief, more than any other facts or reason, makes me brave and fearless as a I am." -**Major-General George Armstrong Custer**

"I think that when God grants me victory over the rest of Palestine I shall divide my territories, make a will stating my wishes, then set sail on this sea for their far-off lands and pursue the Franks there, so as to free the earth of anyone who does not believe in God, or die in the attempt." -**Saladin**

"If I am not in the state of grace, may God put me there; and if I am, may God so keep me." -**Joan of Arc**

"Of the love or hatred God has for the English, I know nothing, but I do know that they will all be thrown out of France, except those who die there." -**Joan of Arc**

"King of England, and you duke of Bedford... give up to the Maid sent here by the King of Heaven the key of all the noble cities of France you have taken and ravaged... I have come here... to drive you man for man from France... If you will not believe the Maid's message from God, wherever you happen to be we... shall make such a great hahaye as has not been made in France these thousand years."-**Joan of Arc**

"I was the first to set a ladder against the fortress on the bridge, and, as I raised it, I was wounded in the throat by a cross-bow bolt. But Saint Catherine comforted me greatly, and I did not cease to ride and do my work." -**Joan of Arc**

"You say that you are my judge. I do not know if you are! But I tell you that you must take good care not to judge me wrongly, because you will put yourself in great danger. I warn you, so that if God punishes you for it, I would have done my duty by telling you!" -**Joan of Arc**

"Hope in God. If you have good hope and faith in him, you shall be delivered from your enemies." -**Joan of Arc**

*Inquisitor:* "Did you ask your saints if, by virtue of your banner, you would win every battle you entered, and be victorious?"

*Joan:* "They told me to take it up bravely and God would help me."

*Inquisitor:* "Which helped you more - you your banner, or your banner you?"

*Joan:* "As to whether victory was my banner's or mine, it was all our Lords's."
**-Joan of Arc**


"You have been with your council and I have been with mine. Believe me that the counsel of my Lord will be accomplished and will stand, and the counsel of yours will perish." **-Joan of Arc**


"Lo, There Do I See My Father,

Lo, There Do I See My Mother,

My Sisters And My Brothers,

Lo, There Do I See My People,

Back To The Beginning,

Lo, There Do They Call To Me,

And Beg Me To Take My Place,

In The Halls Of Valhalla,

Where the Brave Shall Live Forever." **-Norsemen Battle Prayer**

# Chapter 8
# Miscellaneous but Memorable

*S*ome good or famous quotes aren't easy to pigeonhole, but are well worth recording and remembering. These range from the quirky and the curious to the pithy. Sometimes, it's the situation that makes a saying memorable. *"Come and take them,"* might sound like your mother telling you that your dinner's ready, but the everyday phrase has a lot more memorable impact when said by Leonidas of Sparta at the head of a handful of Spartans to the commander of the vast Persian army demanding that the Spartans lay down their weapons – the Spartans were famous for this sort of blunt, brief repartee, known as *"Laconic wit"*. A number of the quotes in this chapter are in a similar spirit: brave, gallant defiance that laughs in the face of danger. Others are less easy to categorize, but are worth it!

---

"It is good that war is so horrible, or we might grow to like it." -**Robert E. Lee**

"The only way human beings can win a war is to prevent it." -**George Marshall**

"The superior fighter has won before engaging in battle." -**Jiang Taigong**

"The enemy is in front of us, the enemy is behind us, the enemy is to the right and to the left of us. They can't get away this time!" -**Douglas MacArthur**

"If fighting is sure to result in victory, then you must fight, even though the ruler forbid it; if fighting will not result in victory, then you must not fight even at the ruler's bidding." -**Sun Tzu**

"But further, to a victory obtained in war attaches a far greater weight of glory than belongs to the noblest contest of the arena." -**Xenophon**

"Let it be thy earnest and incessant care as a Roman and a man to perform whatsoever it is that thou art about, with true and unfeigned gravity, natural affection, freedom and justice: and as for all other cares, and imaginations, how thou mayest ease thy mind of them. Which thou shalt do; if thou shalt go about every action as thy last action, free from all vanity, all passionate and wilful aberration from reason, and from all hypocrisy, and self-love, and dislike of those things, which by the fates or appointment of God have happened unto thee. Thou seest that those things, which for a man to hold on in a prosperous course, and to live a divine life, are requisite and necessary, are not many, for the gods will require no more of any man, that shall but keep and observe these things." -**Marcus Aurelius**

"A man whose passion was war. When he could have kept at peace without shame or damage, he chose war; when he could have been idle, he wished for hard work that he might have war; when he could have kept wealth without danger, he chose to make it less by making war; there was a man who spent upon war as if it were a darling lover or some other pleasure." -**Xenophon, describing the Spartan mercenary general Clearchus.**

"We are not retreating – we are advancing in another direction." -**Douglas MacArthur**

"My saddle is my council chamber." -**Saladin**

"When God gave me the land of Egypt", said he, "I was sure that He meant Palestine for me also." -**Saladin**

"All arts and trades whatever are brought to perfection by continual practice. How much more should this maxim, true in inconsiderable matters, be observed in affairs of importance! And how much superior to all others is the art of war, by which our liberties are preserved, our dignities perpetuated and the provinces and the whole Empire itself exist." -**Publius Flavius Vegetius Renatus**

"I have just returned from visiting the Marines at the front, and there is not a finer fighting organization in the world!" -**Douglas MacArthur**

"A ship without Marines is like a garment without buttons."
-**Rear Admiral David Dixon Porter**

"O divine art of subtlety and secrecy! Through you we learn to be invisible, through you inaudible; and hence we can hold the enemy's fate in our hands." -**Sun Tzu**

"Men willingly believe what they wish." -**Julius Caesar**

"Under God, our troopers, if properly cared for, are the finer men; our infantry of the line are no less numerous, and as regards physique, if it comes to that, not one whit inferior, while in reference to moral qualities, they are more susceptible to the spur of a noble ambition, if only under God's will they be correctly trained. Or again, as touching pride of ancestry, what have Athenians to fear as against Boeotians on that score?"
-**Xenophon**

"All overconfidence, as most pernicious in its consequences, must be banished from the deliberations." **-Publius Flavius Vegetius Renatus**

"I have seen him [the Old Man of the Mountains] — and that is very different from hearing of him." **-Saladin**

"To seek what is impossible is madness." **-Marcus Aurelius**

"They say I am a boy. I am coming to teach them that I am a man."
**-Alexander the Great, prior to the siege of Thebes.**

"If you wish to communicate with me on any subject hereafter, I shall pay no attention to what you send unless you address it to me as your king." **-Alexander the Great**

"It is not the custom of kings to slay kings; but that man had transgressed all bounds, so what happened, happened." **-Saladin**

"Give thyself leisure to learn some good thing, and cease roving and wandering to and fro." **-Marcus Aurelius**

"It is only one who is thoroughly acquainted with the evils of war that can thoroughly understand the profitable way of carrying it on." **-Sun Tzu**

"We have plain bread and meat, and eat it when we are hungry; so we get health and strength,and have very little trouble." **-Cyrus the Great**

"That which does no harm to the state, does no harm to the citizen. In the case of every appearance of harm apply this rule: if the state is not harmed by this, neither am I harmed. But if the state is harmed, thou must not be angry with him who does harm to the state. Show him where his error is." **-Marcus Aurelius**

"Hope!" **-Alexander the Great, in reply to a question about what booty and spoils he reserved for himself rather than distributing to his friends.**

"Come on, you sons of bitches – do you want to live forever?"
**-Gunnery Sergeant Dan Daly, USMC, Belleau Wood**

"Come on Lakotas! It's a good day to die! **-Crazy Horse, rallying the Lakota warriors to defend their camp on Little Big Horn River against Custer's attack.**

"O Men, rejoice at good tidings! God is well-pleased with what ye have done, and this is the summit of man's desire; he hath help you to bring back this strayed camel from misguided hands and to restore it to the fold of Islam, after the infidels had mishandled it for nearly a hundred years."   **-Saladin, on the successful conquest of Jerusalem.**

"Hard pressed on my right. My center is yielding. Impossible to maneuver. Situation excellent. I am attacking!"  **-Ferdinand Foch**

"The more Marines I have around, the better I like it!" **-Gen. Mark Clark**

"How cruel it is not to allow men to strive after the things which appear to them to be suitable to their nature and profitable!" **-Marcus Aurelius**

"One person can make a difference and every person should try." **-John F Kennedy**

"I consider these wounds a blessing; they were given me for some good and wise purpose, and I would not part with them if I could." **-Stonewall Jackson, speaking from his deathbed after the Battle of Chancellorsville.**

"To the strongest." **-Alexander the Great, answering the question who he would leave his empire after his death.**

"Impossible is a word to be found only in the dictionary of fools."
**-Napoleon Bonaparte**

"In the practical art of war, the best thing of all is to take the enemy's country whole and intact; to shatter and destroy it is not so good. So, too, it is better to recapture an army entire than to destroy it, to capture a regiment, a detachment or a company entire than to destroy them." **-Sun Tzu**

"Victory in war is the main object in war. If this is long delayed, weapons are blunted and morale depressed..." **-Sun Tzu**

"Our life is a warfare and a mere pilgrimage. Fame after life is no better than oblivion."
**-Marcus Aurelius**

"I have destroyed [the Thebans'] city, and they have a right to consider me their enemy, and to do all they can to oppose my progress, and to regain their own lost existence and their former power." **-Alexander the Great**

"Glory is fleeting, but obscurity is forever." **-Napoleon Bonaparte**

"Come and take them!" -**King Leonidas of Sparta to Xerxes before the battle of Thermopylae after a request that the Spartans lay down their weapons.**

"No great dependence is to be placed on the eagerness of young soldiers for action, for fighting has something agreeable in the idea to those who are strangers to it."
-**Publius Flavius Vegetius Renatus**

"If it cost me my throne, I will bury the world under its ruins!"
-**Napoleon Bonaparte**

"The army is the true nobility of our country." -**Napoleon Bonaparte**

"Live for something rather than die for nothing." -**General Patton**

"May God have mercy upon my enemies, because I won't." -**General Patton**

"Neither the labor which the hand does nor that of the foot is contrary to nature, so long as the foot does the foot's work and the hand the hand's." -**Marcus Aurelius**

"All glory is fleeting." -**General Patton, (echoing Napoleon)**

"To see victory only when it is within the ken of the common herd is not the acme of excellence." -**Sun Tzu**

"It is not sufficient that I succeed – all others must fail." -**Genghis Khan**

"One does not sell the earth upon which the people walk." -**Crazy Horse**

"My lands are where my dead lie buried." -**Crazy Horse**

"Another white man's trick! Let me go! Let me die fighting!" -**Crazy Horse**

"A very great vision is needed, and the man who has it must follow it as the eagle seeks the deepest blue of the sky." -**Crazy Horse**

"When I was a boy the Sioux owned the world; the sun rose and set on their land; they sent ten thousand men to battle. Where are the warriors today? Who slew them? Where are their lands? Who owns them?" -**Sitting Bull**

"Retreat Hell! We're just attacking in another direction." -**Oliver P. Smith**

"I might yield to the conqueror, and have him assign to me some province or kingdom to govern as his subordinate; but I will never submit to such a degradation. I can die in the struggle, but never will yield. I will wear no crown which another puts upon my brow, nor give up my right to reign over the empire of my ancestors till I give up my life." -**King Darius III of Persia**

"If we do not wish to fight, we can prevent the enemy from engaging us even though the lines of our encampment be merely traced out on the ground. All we need do is to throw something odd and unaccountable in his way." -**Sun Tzu**

"War takes away the easy supply of daily wants, and so proves a rough master, that brings most men's characters to a level with their fortunes." -**Thucydides**

"Eat well, for tonight we dine in Hades." -**Leonidas, before the battle of Thermopylae.**

"Liberty will not be kept, but men shall be trodden underfoot and brought to most horrible misery and calamity if they, giving themselves to pastimes and pleasure, forsake the just regard of their own defense and safeguard of their country, which... chiefly consists in warlike skilfulness." -**Machiavelli**

"The idle business of show, plays on the stage, flocks of sheep, herds, exercises with spears, a bone cast to little dogs, a bit of bread into fishponds, laborings of ants and burden-carrying, runnings about of frightened little mice, puppets pulled by strings – they are all alike. It is thy duty then in the midst of such things to show good humor and not a proud air; to understand however that every man is worth just so much as the things are worth about which he busies himself." -**Marcus Aurelius**

"What the ancients called a clever fighter is one who not only wins, but excels in winning with ease." -**Sun Tzu**

*"Uri, Vinciri, Verberari, Ferroque Necari"* (I will endure, to be burned, to be bound, to be beaten, and to be killed by the sword) -**Sacramentum gladiatorium, the oath of the gladiators.**

*"Veni, Vidi, Vici."* (I came, I saw, I conquered.) -**Julius Caesar**

*"Iacta alea est."* (The die is cast.) -**Julius Caesar, crossing the Rubicon river with his troops, thus declaring war on the Roman senate.**

*"Semper Fidelis"* (Always Faithful) -**Motto of the U.S. Marine Corps.**

*"De oppresso liber"* (To Liberate The Oppressed) -**Motto of the U.S Army Special Forces.**

"Who dares wins." **-Motto of the Special Air Services (SAS).**

"I don't believe we can have an army without music." **-Robert E. Lee**

"No bastard ever won a war by dying for his country. He won it by making the other poor dumb bastard die for his country." **-General Patton**

"The first and last essential of an efficient soldier is character; without it he will not long endure the perils of modern war." **-Lord Moran**

"War is a conflict of great interests which is settled by bloodshed, and only in that is it different from others." **-Karl von Clausewitz**

"The best way to quiet a country is a good thrashing, followed by great kindness afterwards. Even the wildest chaps are thus tamed." **-Sir Charles Napier**

"The bloody solution of the crisis, the effort for the destruction of the enemy's forces, is the first-born son of war." **-Karl von Clausewitz**

"We have met the enemy and they are ours..." **-Oliver Hazard Perry**

"Every man dies. Not every man really lives." **-William Wallace**

"I can not be a traitor, for I owe him no allegiance. He is not my Sovereign; he never received my homage; and whilst life is in this persecuted body, he never shall receive it."
**-William Wallace**

"If I or my soldiers have plundered or done injury to the houses or ministers of religion, I repent me of my sin; but it is not of Edward of England I shall ask pardon."
**-William Wallace**

"We come here with no peaceful intent, but ready for battle, determined to avenge our wrongs and set our country free." **-William Wallace**

"Freedom is best, I tell thee true, of all things to be won." **-William Wallace**

"I have brought you to the ring; hop [dance] if you can." **-William Wallace**

"The greatest joy for a man is to defeat his enemies, to drive them before him, to take from them all they possess, to see those they love in tears, to ride their horses, and to hold their wives and daughters in his arms." **-Genghis Khan**

"In war, numbers alone confer no advantage." **-Sun Tzu**

"Damn the torpedoes, Full speed ahead!" **-Admiral David Glasgow Farragut**

"Moreover, when an ant is struck, does it not fight back and bite the hand of the man that struck it?" **-Labayu**

"Liberty, when it begins to take root, is a plant of rapid growth." **-George Washington**

"Pain is neither intolerable nor everlasting, if thou bearest in mind that it has its limits, and if thou addest nothing to it in imagination." **-Marcus Aurelius**

"Am I not destroying my enemies when I make friends of them?" **-Abraham Lincoln**

"I am still puzzled as to how far the individual counts; a lot, I fancy, if he pushes the right way." **-Lawrence of Arabia**

"I am an optimist. It does not seem to much use being anything else."
**-Winston Churchill**

"War is a science for those who are outstanding; an art for mediocrities; a trade for ignoramuses." **-Frederick the Great**

"Riches do not consist in the possession of treasures but in the use of them."
**-Napoleon Bonaparte**

"It is not fit that I should give myself pain, for I have never intentionally given pain even to another." **-Marcus Aurelius**

"War is always a matter of doing evil in the hope that some good may come of it."
**-Captain Sir Basil Liddell Hart**

"Battle is the bloodiest solution. While it should not simply be considered as mutual murder - its effect... is rather a killing of the enemy's spirit than of his men - it is always true that the character of a battle, like its name, is slaughter (Schlacht), and its price is blood." **-Karl von Clausewitz**

"When I look back on all these worries, I remember the story of the old man who said on his deathbed that he had had a lot of trouble in his life, most of which had never happened." **-Winston Churchill**

"Wilson, I am a damned sight smarter than Grant. I know a great deal more about war, military history, strategy, and grand tactics than he does; I know more about organization, supply, and administration, and about everything else than he does. But I tell you where he beats me, and where he beats the world. He don't care a damn for what the enemy does out of his sight, but it scares me like hell... I am more nervous than he is. I am more likely to change my orders, or to countermarch my command than he is. He uses such information as he has, according to his best judgment. He issues his orders and does his level best to carry them out without much reference to what is going on about him." **-General Tecumseh Sherman**

"In discourse thou must attend to what is said, and in every movement thou must observe what is doing. And in the one thou shouldst see immediately to what end it refers, but in the other watch carefully what is the thing signified." **-Marcus Aurelius**

"We've been looking for the enemy for some time now. We've finally found him. We're surrounded. That simplifies things." **-Lewis Burwell "Chesty" Puller**

"The people of London with one voice would say to Hitler: 'You have committed every crime under the sun… We will have no truce or parley with you, or the grisly gang who work your wicked will.  You do your worst – and we will do our best."
**-Winston Churchill**

"I cannot forecast to you the action of Russia.  It is a riddle wrapped in a mystery inside an enigma." **-Winston Churchill**

"Speak both in the senate and to every man, whoever he may be, appropriately, not with any affectation: use plain discourse." **-Marcus Aurelius**

"My men have turned into women; my women into men." **-Xerxes, commenting on the fighting prowess of Artemisia, in contrast to his male naval commanders.**

"There are five reasons why wars are started and they are: to contend for fame; to contend for benefits and advantages; to seek revenge; and internal strife and from famine. The names of wars raised based on these reasons are: righteous, bully, anger, plundering, contrary.

The 'righteous' army is raised to save people from chaos. Relying on strength or power to bully people, such is the 'bully' army. Mobilising the army out of anger is termed as 'anger' army. Army raised to greedily seek profit without consideration for moral and ethics is called a 'plundering' army. While the country is in turmoil and the people are exhausted, embarking on military campaigns and mobilizing the masses is termed 'contrary'.

There are appropriate strategies to counter these wars. In the case of the 'righteous', you must use propriety to subjugate them. For the 'bully' you must be deferential to subjugate them. Against the 'anger' army, you must use verbal persuasion to subjugate them. Against the 'plundering' army you must win them with wits. Against the 'contrary', you must strictly impose your authority to subjugate them." -**Wu Qi**


"War is too serious a matter to entrust to military men." -**Georges Clemenceau**


"Politics is war without bloodshed while war is politics with bloodshed." -**Mao Zedong**


"My dear Excellency! I have not gone to war to collect cheese and eggs, but for another purpose." -**Manfred von Richthofen**


"If the Persians hide the sun [by shooting such vast numbers of arrows], we shall have our battle in the shade." -**Dieneces**


"It is in truth not for glory, nor riches, nor honours that we are fighting, but for freedom – for that alone, which no honest man gives up but with life itself." -**Robert the Bruce**, **Declaration of Arbroath.**

"It is easier to make war than to make peace." **-Georges Clemeceau**

"Out there among you are the cynics, the people who scoff at what you're learning here. The people that scoff at character, the people that scoff at hard work. But they don't know what they're talking about, let me tell you. I can assure you that when the going gets tough and your country needs them, they're not going to be there. They will not be there, but you will... After Vietnam, we had a whole cottage industry develop basically in Washington, D.C., that consisted of a bunch of military fairies that had never been shot at in anger, who felt fully qualified to comment on the leadership ability of all the leaders of the United States Army. They were not Monday morning quarterbacks, they were the worst of all possible kind, they were Friday afternoon quarterbacks. They felt qualified to criticize us even before the game was played... And they are the same people who are saying, my good-ness, we have terrible problems in the armed forces because there are no more leaders out there, there are no more combat leaders. Where are the Eisen-howers? Where are the Bradleys? Where are the MacArthurs? Where are the Audie Murphys?... Coming from a guy who's never been shot at in his entire life, that's a pretty bold statement." **-General Norman Schwarzkopf, addressing the Cadets at West Point.**

"War without fire is like sausages without mustard." **-Henry V**

"Sire, there are enough to kill, enough to capture and enough to run away." **-Report by a squire to Henry V on the size of the French army.**

"But does any man among you honestly feel that he has suffered more for me than I have suffered for him? Come now - if you are wounded, strip and show your wounds, and I will show mine. There is no part of my body but my back which has not a scar; not a-weapon a man may grasp or fling the mark of which I do not carry upon me. I have sword-cuts from close fight; arrows have pierced me, missiles from catapults bruised my flesh; again and again I have been struck by stones or clubs - and all for your sakes: for your glory and gain." **-Alexander the Great**

"The wind commands me away." -**Sir Francis Drake**

"There is plenty of time to win this game, and to thrash the Spaniards too."
-**Sir Francis Drake**

"There is no feeling more central to our being than the desire for freedom.  From people that are most organized to those that are most barbarian, all are penetrated by it; because, as we are born without chains, we demand to live without constraint.  It is this spirit of independence and pride which produced so many great men in the world."
-**Frederick the Great**

"You cannot exaggerate about the Marines. They are convinced to the point of arrogance, that they are the most ferocious fighters on earth - and the amusing thing about it is that they are."  -**Father Kevin Keaney, 1st Marine Division Chaplain in the Korean War.**

"Before this time tomorrow, I shall have gained a peerage or Westminster Abbey."
-**Horatio Nelson on the eve of the Battle of the Nile.**

"My first wish is, to see this plague of mankind banished from the earth, and the sons and daughters of this world employed in more pleasing and innocent amusements, than in preparing implements, and exercising them, for the destruction of mankind."
-**George Washington**

"The deadliest weapon in the world is a Marine and his rifle!" -**General Pershing**

"Is life so dear, or peace so sweet, as to be purchased at the price of chains and slavery? Forbid it, Almighty God!  I know not what course others may take, but as for me, give me liberty or give me death!"  -**Patrick Henry**

"The trials we have had show that the rebels [the American colonist militiamen] are not the despicable rabble too many have supposed them to be, and I find it owing to a military spirit encouraged among them for a few years past, joined with an uncommon degree of zeal and enthusiasm, that they are otherwise." -**General Gage**

"You know, Foley, I have only one eye – I have a right to be blind sometimes... I really do not see the signal." -**Horatio Nelson, ignoring a signal to retreat.**

"I do not say they cannot come. I only say they cannot come by sea."
-**Admiral Earl St Vincent**

"I don't know what effect these men will have upon the enemy, but, by God, they frighten me!" -**Sir Arthur Wellesley, Duke of Wellington**

"In order to have good soldiers, a nation must always be at war." - **Napoleon Bonaparte**

"Northern politicians do not appreciate the determination and pluck of the South, and Southern politicians do not appreciate the numbers, resources, and patient perseverance of the North. Both sides forget that we are all Americans, and that it must be a terrible struggle if it comes to war." -**Robert E. Lee**

"You might as well attempt to put out the flames of a burning house with a squirt-gun. I think this is to be a long war – very long – much longer than any politician thinks."
-**Colonel William T Sherman**

"We are advocates of the abolition of war, we do not want war; but war can only be abolished through war, and in order to get rid of the gun it is necessary to take up the gun." -**Mao Zedong**

"They [the young soldiers of the South] are the most dangerous set of men that this war has turned loose upon the world. They are splendid riders, first-rate shots and utterly reckless... These men must all be killed or employed by us before we can hope for peace." -**Colonel William T Sherman**

"If a man consults whether he is to fight, when he has the power in his own hands, it is certain that his opinion is against fighting." -**Horatio Nelson**

"I propose to fight it out on this line if it takes all summer." -**Ulysses S. Grant**

"It is the duty of the officers of the legion, of the tribunes, and even of the commander-in-chief himself, to take care that the sick soldiers are supplied with proper diet and diligently attended by the physicians. For little can be expected from men who have both the enemy and diseases to struggle with. However, the best judges of the service have always been of the opinion that daily practice of the military exercises is much more efficacious towards the health of an army than all the art of medicine."
-**Publius Flavius Vegetius Renatus**

"There are a lot of men howling about their rights who have never done anything to earn any rights. Do your duty first and you will get your rights afterwards."
-**Robert Baden-Powell**

"Russia has two generals whom she can trust: General Janiver [January] and General Fevrier [February]." -**Tsar Nicholas I, on the defeat of Napoleon's army besieging Moscow during the winter.**

"It is better to offer no excuse than a bad one." -**George Washington**

"Good officers never engage in general actions unless induced by opportunity or obliged by necessity." -**Publius Flavius Vegetius Renatus**

"Trust is a distinguished reward for warriors." -**Sun Bin**

"An army, in fact, tries to work together in a battle or a large maneuver in much the same way as a football team plays together in a match... The army fights for the good of its country as the team plays for the honor of the school... "Exceptionally gallant charges and heroic defences correspond to brilliant runs and fine tackling."
-**Frederick Gordon Guggisberg**

"Battle is an orgy of disorder. No level lawns or marker flags exist to aid us strut ourselves in vain display, but rather groups of weary wandering men seek gropingly for means to kill their foe. The sudden change from accustomed order to utter disorder - to chaos, but emphasize the folly of schooling to precision and obedience where only fierceness and habituated disorder are useful." -**General Patton**

"The dominant feeling of the battlefield is loneliness." -**Field Marshal Viscount Slim of Burma**

"War is hell." -**General Tecumseh Sherman**

"There is many a boy today who looks on war as all glory, but, boys, it is all hell. You can hear this warning voice to generations yet to come. I look upon war with horror."
-**General Tecumseh Sherman**

"You people of the South don't know what you are doing. This country will be drenched in blood, and God only knows how it will end. It is all folly, madness, a crime against civilization! You people speak so lightly of war; you don't know what you're talking about. War is a terrible thing!" -**General Tecumseh Sherman**

"I am a damned sight smarter man than Grant. I know more about military history, strategy, and grand tactics than he does. I know more about supply, administration, and everything else than he does. I'll tell you where he beats me though and where he beats the world. He doesn't give a damn about what the enemy does out of his sight, but it scares me like hell." -**General Tecumseh Sherman**

"I confess, without shame, that I am sick and tired of fighting - its glory is all moonshine; even success the most brilliant is over dead and mangled bodies, with the anguish and lamentations of distant families, appealing to me for sons, husbands, and fathers ... it is only those who have never heard a shot, never heard the shriek and groans of the wounded and lacerated ... that cry aloud for more blood, more vengeance, more desolation." -**General Tecumseh Sherman**

"A professional soldier understands that war means killing people, war means maiming people, war means families left without fathers and mothers. All you have to do is hold your first dying soldier in your arms, and have that terribly futile feeling that his life is flowing out and you can't do anything about it. Then you understand the horror of war."
- **General Norman Schwarzkopf**

"Dost thou wish to be praised by a man who curses himself thrice every hour? Wouldst thou wish to please a man who does not please himself? Does a man please himself who repents of nearly everything that he does?" -**Marcus Aurelius**

"To die for Emperor and Nation is the highest hope of a military man. After a brave hard fight the blossoms are scattered on the fighting field. But if a person wants to take a life instead, still the fighting man will go to eternity for Emperor and country. One man's life or death is a matter of no importance. All that matters is the Empire. As Confucius said, "They may crush cinnabar, yet they do not take away its color; one may burn a fragrant herb, yet it will not destroy the scent." They may destroy my body, yet they will not take away my will." -**Admiral Isoroku Yamamoto**

"The splendor of the arms has no inconsiderable effect in striking terror into an enemy. Can that man be reckoned a good soldier who through negligence suffers his arms to be spoiled by dirt and rust?" -**Publius Flavius Vegetius Renatus**

"A battle that you win cancels any other bad action of yours. In the same way, by losing one, all the good things worked by you before become vain." -**Machiavelli**

"A prisoner of war is a man who tries to kill you and fails, and then asks you not to kill him." -**Winston Churchill**

"Do not despise death, but be well content with it, since this too is one of those things which nature wills." -**Marcus Aurelius**

"Political power grows out of the barrel of a gun." -**Mao Zedong**

"When another blames thee or hates thee, or when men say about thee anything injurious, approach their poor souls, penetrate within, and see what kind of men they are. Thou wilt discover that there is no reason to take any trouble that these men may have this or that opinion about thee." -**Marcus Aurelius**

"What a cruel thing is war; to separate and destroy families and friends, and mar the purest joys and happiness God has granted us in this world; to fill our hearts with hatred instead of love for our neighbours, and to devastate the fair face of this beautiful world." -**Robert E. Lee**

"A man's worth is no greater than the worth of his ambitions." -**Marcus Aurelius**

"You say that it is your custom to burn widows. Very well. We also have a custom: when men burn a woman alive, we tie a rope around their necks and we hang them. Build your funeral pyre; [then] beside it, my carpenters will build a gallows. You may follow your custom. And then we will follow ours." -**Sir Charles Napier, on the Indian custom of suttee.**

"Nuts!" -**General Anthony McAuliffe, in response to a German demand to surrender.**

"It is a ridiculous thing for a man not to fly from his own badness, which is indeed possible, but [it is ridiculous] to fly from other men's badness, which is impossible." -**Marcus Aurelius**

"So long as you are a slave to the opinions of the many you have not yet approached freedom or tasted its nectar." -**Flavius Claudius Julianus**

"Zeal to do all that is in one's power is, in truth, a proof of piety." - **Flavius Claudius Julianus**

"Men should be taught and won over by reason, not by blows, insults, and corporal punishments." -**Flavius Claudius Julianus**

"A lie gets halfway around the world before the truth has a chance to get its pants on." -**Winston Churchill**

"We have known the bitterness of defeat and the exultation of triumph, and from both we have learned there can be no turning back. We must go forward to preserve in peace what we won in war." -**Douglas MacArthur**

"Mortal danger is an effective antidote for fixed ideas." -**Erwin Rommel**

"On the occasion of every act ask thyself: How is this with respect to me? Shall I repent of it? A little time and I am dead, and all is gone. What more do I seek, if what I am now doing is the work of an intelligent living being, and a social being, and one who is under the same law with God?" -**Marcus Aurelius**

"Let us therefore animate and encourage each other, and show the whole world that a Freeman, contending for liberty on his own ground, is superior to any slavish mercenary on earth." -**George Washington**

"Our enemies are Medes and Persians, men who for centuries have lived soft and luxurious lives; we of Macedon for generations past have been trained in the hard school of danger and war." -**Alexander the Great**

"I have with me two gods, Persuasion and Compulsion." -**Themistocles**

"Sex and sleep alone make me conscious that I am mortal." -**Alexander the Great**

"Indeed I have observed that even the Barbarians across the Rhine sing savage songs composed in language not unlike the croaking of harsh-voiced birds, and that they delight in such songs. For I think it is always the case that inferior musicians, though they annoy their audiences, give very great pleasure to themselves."
-**Flavius Claudius Julianus**

"Ideals are like stars; you will not succeed in touching them with your hands. But like the seafaring man on the desert of waters, you choose them as your guides, and following them you will reach your destiny." -**Carl Schurz**

"The survival of this country depends upon letting the world know we have the power and the ability to use it if the occasion demands." -**Forrest Sherman**

"Leave this world a little better than you found it." -**Robert Baden-Powell**

"Up! Children of Zulu, your day has come. Up! And destroy them all!" -**Shaka Zulu**

"The most powerful weapon on earth is the human soul on fire." -**Ferdinand Foch**

"Nothing is more exhilarating than to be shot at without result." -**Winston Churchill**

"When a thing is done, it's done. Don't look back. Look forward to your next objective." -**George Marshall**

"I may be accused of rashness but not of sluggishness." -**Napoleon Bonaparte**

"As long as our government is administered for the good of the people, and is regulated by their will; as long as it secures to us the rights of persons and of property, liberty of conscience, and of the press, it will be worth defending." -**Andrew Jackson**

"I read, I study, I examine, I listen, I reflect, and out of all of this I try to form an idea into which I put as much common sense as I can." -**Gilbert du Motier, marquis de La Fayette**

"I love war and responsibility and excitement. Peace is going to be hell on me." -**General Patton**

"This is the Way for men who want to learn my strategy:

Do not think dishonestly.

The Way is in training.

Become acquainted with every art.

Know the Ways of all professions.

Distinguish between gain and loss in worldly matters.

Develop intuitive judgment and understanding for everything.

Perceive those things which cannot be seen.

Pay attention even to trifles.

Do nothing which is of no use." -**Miyamoto Musashi**

"The rank of Officers, which to me, Sir, is much dearer than the Pay."
-**George Washington**

"Men rise from one ambition to another: First, they seek to secure themselves against attack, and then they attack others." -**Machiavelli**

"Climate is what you expect but weather is what you get." -**American Military Saying**

"In archery we have three goals: to shoot accurately, to shoot powerfully, to shoot rapidly." -**Anonymous Byzantine General**

"I do not care whether I command a large or a small army; but large or small, I will be obeyed and I will not suffer pillage." -**Sir Arthur Wellesley, The Duke of Wellington**

"The affairs of war, like the destiny of battles, as well of empires, hang upon a spider's thread." -**Napoleon Bonaparte**

"In war there is never any chance for a second mistake." -**Lamachus**

"The man whose profession is arms should calm his mind and look into the depths of others. Doing so is likely the best of the martial arts." -**Shiba Yoshimasa**

"Power for the sake of lording it over fellow creatures or adding to personal pomp, is rightly judged base. But power in a national crisis, when a man believes he knows what orders should be given, is a blessing." -**Winston Churchill**

"Peace is an armistice in a war that is continuously going on." -**Thucydides**

"Happy is that city which in time of peace thinks of war."
-**Inscription in the Armoury of Venice.**

"Four hostile newspapers were more to be feared than a thousand bayonets."
-**Napoleon Bonaparte**

"I like only those who make war." -**Napoleon Bonaparte**

"War is the only proper school of the surgeon." -**Hippocrates**

"Strike an enemy once and for all. Let him cease to exist as a tribe or he will live to fly at your throat again." -**Shaka Zulu**

"To those who congratulated him on his victory in the battle against the Arcadians, he said: 'It would be better if our intelligence were beating them rather than our strength.'"
-**Archidamus III**

"Those who despise violence are warriors fit to work for kings." -**Sun Bin**

"Passing through Douclon woods, we , heard the moans of wounded men all around us. It was a gruesome sound. A low voice from a nearby bush called 'Kamerad, Kamerad!' A youngster from the 127th lay with a breast wound on the cold stony ground. The poor lad sobbed as we stooped over him - he did not want to die. We wrapped him in his coat and shelter half, gave him some water, and made him as comfortable as possible. We heard the voices of wounded men on all sides now. One called in a heart-breaking way for his mother. Another prayed. Others were crying with pain and mingled with the voices we heard the sound of French: 'Des blesses, camarade!' It was terrible to listen to suffering and dying men. We helped friend and foe without distinction."
**-Erwin Rommel**

"I heard the bullets whistle, and believe me, there is something charming in the sound."
**-George Washington**

"Don't you think that I have something worth being sorry about, when I reflect that at my age Alexander was already king over so many peoples, while I have never yet achieved anything really remarkable?" **-Julius Caesar**

"I begin to regard the death and mangling of a couple thousand men as a small affair, a kind of morning dash - and it may well be that we become so hardened."
**-General Tecumseh Sherman**

"To be at the head of a strong column of troops, in the execution of some task that requires brain, is the highest pleasure of war - a grim one and terrible, but which leaves on the mind and memory the strongest mark; to detect the weak point of an enemy's line; to break through with vehemence and thus lead to victory; or to discover some key-point and hold it with tenacity; or to do some other distinct act which is afterward recognized as the real cause of success. These all become matters that are never forgotten."
**-General Tecumseh Sherman**

"The most vital quality a soldier can possess is self-confidence, utter, complete and bumptious." -**General Patton**

"Yesterday, December 7, 1941 - a date which will live in infamy - the United States was suddenly and deliberately attacked by the naval and air forces of the empire of Japan...

The facts of yesterday and today speak for themselves. The people of the United States have already formed their opinions and well understand the implications to the very life and safety of our nation.

As Commander-in-Chief of our armed forces, I have directed that all measures be taken for our defense.

Always remember the character of the onslaught against us.

No matter how long it may take us to overcome this premeditated invasion, the American people, in their righteous might, will win through to absolute victory...

With confidence in our armed forces, with the unbounding determination of our people, we will gain the inevitable triumph. So help us God.

I ask that the Congress declare that since the unprovoked and dastardly attack by Japan, on December 7, 1941, a state of war has existed between the United States and the Japanese Empire."-**Franklin D. Roosevelt, asking Congress to declare war on Japan after the attack on Pearl Harbor.**

"All through your career of Army life, you men have bitched about what you call this chicken shit drilling. That is all for one reason, instant obedience to orders and it creates alertness. I don't give a damn for a man who is not always on his toes. You men are veterans or you wouldn't be here. You are ready. A man to continue breathing, must be alert at all times. If not, sometimes, some German son of a bitch will sneak up behind him and beat him to death with a sack full of shit." -**General Patton**

"Battle is not a terrifying ordeal to be endured. It is a magnificent experience wherein all the elements that have made man superior to the beasts are present: courage, self-sacrifice, loyalty, help to others, devotion to duty. As you go in, you will perhaps be a little short of breath, and your knees may tremble... This breathlessness, this tremor, are not fear. It is simply the excitement every athlete feels just before the whistle blows - no, you will not fear for you will be borne up and exhalted by the proud instinct of our conquering race. You will be inspired by a magnificent hate." -**General Patton**

"Most people think Americans love luxury and that their culture is shallow and meaningless. It is a mistake to regard the Americans as luxury-loving and weak. I can tell you Americans are full of the spirit of Justice, fight and adventure. Also their thinking is very advanced and scientific. Lindbergh's solo crossing of the Atlantic is the sort of valiant act which is normal for them. That is typically American adventure based on science." -**Admiral Isoroku Yamamoto**

"No citizen has any right to be an amateur in the matter of physical training. It is part of his profession as a citizen to keep himself in good condition, ready to serve his state at a moment's notice. The instinct of self-preservation demands it likewise: for how helpless is the state of the ill-trained youth in war or in danger! Finally, what a disgrace it is for a man to grow old without ever seeing the beauty and strength of which his body is capable." -**Socrates**

"War justifies everything." -**Napoleon Bonaparte**

"There is no authority without justice." -**Napoleon Bonaparte**

"These three things you must always keep in mind: concentration of strength, activity, and a firm resolve to perish gloriously. These are the three principles of the military art which have disposed luck in all my military operations. Death is nothing, but to live defeated and without glory is to die every day." -**Napoleon Bonaparte**

"In no way should a sworn agreement made with the enemy be broken."
**-The Emperor Maurice**


"You need not imagine that victory will be as hard to win as the fame of our antagonists might suggest. Fortune is fickle: often a despised enemy has fought to the death, and a feather in the scale has brought defeat to famous nations and their kings. Take away the blinding brilliance of the name, and in what can the Romans be compared to you?"
**-Hannibal, addressing his army before the Battle of the Ticinus.**


FOR WANT OF A NAIL...
"For want of a nail the shoe was lost.

For want of a shoe the horse was lost.

For want of a horse the rider was lost.

For want of a rider the battle was lost.

For want of a battle the kingdom was lost.

And all for the want of a horseshoe nail."
**-Traditional English Rhyme**


"There are roads which must not be followed, armies which must not be attacked, towns which must not be besieged, positions which must not be contested, commands of the sovereign which must not be obeyed." **-Sun Tzu**


"Weapons are instruments of ill omen, war is immoral. Really they are only to be resorted to when there is no other choice. It is not right to pursue aggressive warfare because one's country is large and prosperous, for this ultimately ends in defeat and destruction. Then it is too late to have regrets. Military action is like a fire - if not stopped it will burn itself out. Military expansion and adventurism soon lead to disaster. The rule is 'Even if a country is large, if it is militaristic it will eventually perish.'"
**-Liu Ji**

"The sword is the soul of the warrior. If any forget or lose it he will not be excused."
**-Tokugawa Ieyasu**


"The right use of the sword is that it should subdue the barbarians while lying gleaming in its scabbard. If it leaves its sheath it cannot be said to be used rightly. Similarly the right use of military power is that it should conquer the enemy while concealed in the breast. To take the field with an army is to be found wanting in the real knowledge of it. Those who hold the office of Shogun are to be particularly clear on this point."
**-Tokugawa Ieyasu**


"One should not be overly fond of famous swords and daggers. For even if one has a sword valued at 10,000 cash, he will not overcome 100 men carrying spears valued at 100 cash." **-Asakura Toshikage**

# Chapter 9
# Quotes from the Author

*W*hat follows are over 100 maxims which I have developed over the past twenty-five years of instructing the combat arts. They have stood the test of time because they were formed in the heat of battle and formulated in the coolness of reflection. They are here because they helped me help others in their preparations for potential battle in the streets of America. They speak the time-tested truth of real human competition and confrontation. Moreover, they both inspire and instruct and will no doubt be used and re-used by those who have heard them. I modestly hope that they will also lead you through the trials and tribulations of your own struggles and incumbent triumphs.

---

"When danger is imminent, strike first, strike fast and keep the pressure on."

"To truly master the essence of combat, you must study it as a science and express it as an art."

"Approach combat in terms of black and white, but be prepared for gray."

"Never underestimate the vicious capability of a human being."

"Aggressive action wins."

"Every fight must be won fast."

"Life is short, be pragmatic."

"Acquire an insatiable hunger for knowledge."

"Violence begins where diplomacy ends."

"Always treat books with respect and veneration."

"Strict adherence to traditional perspectives will almost guarantee you death in combat."

"Reaching the pinnacle of combative competency does not occur through some mystical transformation. It's acquired through dedication and lots of hard work."

"Beware of the ego. He is a dark beast desirous of destruction."

"If any style or system of combat will not allow for change, then it will surely die."

"Never show an act of defiance that you are not prepared to defend."

"A great warrior will always act swiftly and decisively, he doesn't know the meaning of apprehension."

"A true warrior is always alone."

"Support capital punishment."

"Never teach combat tactics to anyone on the wrong side of the law."

"Frustration and time are the gatekeepers who separate the tyro from the expert."

"In combat, perception is reality."

"The better prepared you are, the less luck you will need."

"Despair is always one step away from death."

"There are no absolutes in combat."

"Train for the exception as well as the rule."

"Order and justice can only be executed through a hand of might."

"Question authority, just do it respectfully."

"You will always have more to lose than your enemy."

"Never betray a friend."

"There is no honor in defeat."

"Never reject a combat tactic simply because you dislike its source."

"Combative truth is not relative."

"For every attack, there is a logical counter."

"Always keep a mindful eye on your own attitude.  It is usually the first thing that will get you into a fight."

"Mankind is getting more violent with the times."

"Humankind is an oxymoron!"

"Anything new creates discomfort."

"Logic changes."

"A well seasoned warrior is an excellent predictor of moves."

"Don't respect pacifists or fight for them."

"Trust no one."

"What you don't know can certainly get you killed in combat."

"Efficiency is <u>not</u> anything that scores."

"A war is never really over."

"Justice is not always served."

"Discover what you don't know."

"The more you know, the less you will fear."

"Success and failure translate to life and death in combat."

"Blind belief and adherence to unproven principles are pure and simple suicide."

"To abandon structure is to abandon the fundamentals of combat."

"Conceptualization shapes and molds combative characteristics, but it becomes useless if it is not solidly and safely actualized."

"Concrete combat systems and strategies provide efficiency and overall combative direction."

"A formidable fighter is a cold and vicious animal, albeit an intelligent one."

"A functional combat system always in a state of genesis."

"Analyze everything!"

"Self-mastery separates the true expert from the eternal novice."

"Beware of the call of violence and be ever vigilant of the ego's charms."

"Combative formlessness is the fetus of death."

"A warrior must police his skills with a moral fabric called honor."

"Fear is established when ignorance is actualized."

"Defend the weak!"

"Every man is afraid of something."

"Acquire the courage and insight to question and change combative paradigms."

"Experimentation in the face of danger is an invitation to disaster."

"It takes a lifetime to master a credible system of combat."

"What's practical isn't always popular, and what's popular isn't always practical."

"Those who instruct, learn."

"Never teach a student everything you know about combat."

"Tactics can be studied. techniques can be learned. but fighting must be experienced."

"In combat, everyone loses in the game of conceptual abstraction."

"Violence is a dark cloak that you  must wear even if you don't like the way it fits."

"As long as mankind walks the earth, there will always be a time, need, and place for combat."

"Life betrays everyone."

"If luck factors in to your formula, then you are still not prepared for combat."

"Every problem has a solution."

"In combat, anything that can go wrong, might go wrong."

"The first casualty of combat is the ego."

"Never, ever forgive evil!"

"Those who speak the truth are never liked."

"Cowards make the best bullies."

"It is far better to die by your own theory than to die by someone elses."

"Leave nothing to chance."

"A true innovator creates for himself and no one else."

"There are two types of people in this world: victims and victors. Which one are you?"

"The only thing that stands between you and death is your ability to fight well."

"You will never know all there is to know."

"Live everyday as if it were your last."

"All great warriors are  slaves of perfection."

"Make sure you know the laws and rules of combat before you attempt to criticize them."

"Self-defense is not just a right. it's your responsibility."

"The truth is always revolutionary."

"It is always better to act than react."

"Truth gives you the power to make things better."

"Nothing is sacred in combat."

"The longer a battle lasts, the greater your chances of injury or death."

"Attack even when you retreat."

"Those who reject the necessity of violence reject the necessity of peace."

"Fools rush into combat."

"Respect rank!"

"While combative preparedness is critical to your survival, never forget the importance of love, life, and laughter."

"Never forget God."

"I believe in God, I just don't believe what men say about God."

"I prefer animals over people, after all their loyalty is never in question."

"You will never know the meaning of true loyalty until you own a dog."

"When your mind, body and spirit fuse into an efficient and unemotional weapon, you will become the warrior."

"Revenge can be an honorable trait."

"Civility is a sweet poison that must be lanced and exorcised if you are ever to become the War Machine."

"Cold indifference drenches my face,

As blue heavens turn to dust,

I am banished by the human race,

For my dark soul craves violent lust,

Oh grant me this rightful dream of hate,

In which flesh and bone sear with pain,

The clock ticks on until its too late,

And those who oppose me lie fallen slain."

**-War Machine Chronicles (Chapter XX, Verse 3)**

# Biographies

## Alexander the Great

Alexander the Great (356–323 BC) is considered to be one of the most successful military commanders of all time. He was king of Macedonia and conqueror of the Persian Empire.

## Archilochus

Archilochus (680 BC–645 BC) was a mercenary warrior and poet of Classical Greek times who is best known as the pioneer of the Lyric style of poetry. One of his poems was used as a hymn in the ancient Olympic Games.

## Arthur

Arthur was a legendary British leader who fought against the Saxon invasion in the early 6th century. The historical Arthur became the hero of many legends, which referred to him as "King Arthur". He is considered to be one of the greatest heroes of Celtic (especially Welsh) culture.

## Sir Jacob Astley

Sir Jacob Astley (1579–1652) was a commander of the Royalist troops supporting Charles I during the English Civil War.

## Marcus Aurelius

Marcus Aurelius Antoninus (121–180 AD) was a Roman emperor and philosopher, who is known as one of the "Five Good Emperors", because his personal character contrasted with the decadence and corruption of other emperors. Marcus Aurelius undertook numerous campaigns to stabilize the Roman Empire, especially in Germany. During this campaign, Marcus Aurelius wrote a philosophical treatise known as the *Meditations*. He is considered to be an excellent example of the philosopher-king of the Platonic tradition.

## Robert Baden-Powell

Robert Baden-Powell (1857–1941) was a lieutenant-general in the British Army and founder of the Boy Scouts movement. He wrote the manual *"Scouting for Boys"* outlining the principles of honor, discipline and tactics, often drawing on his experiences in the field.

## Beowulf

Beowulf was probably a fictional warrior of the Scandinavians and Germanic peoples of the time. He is the hero of a long Anglo-Saxon poem.

## Major Frederick Blesse

Major General Frederick C. "Boots" Blesse was considered a Korean War Fighter Pilot Ace. He flew F-86 Sabre jets for USAF and downed 9 MiGs. He wrote *"No Guts, No Glory,"* a fighter pilot manual.

## Tsukahara Bokuden

Tsukahara Bokuden (1489–1571) was a famous Samurai swordsman during the early Sengoku period. Born into the upper classes, he was widely regarded as a kensei (sword saint) and founded a new discipline of fencing.

## Napoleon Bonaparte

Napoleon Bonaparte's full title was Emperor Napoleon Bonaparte, Napoleon 1st of France (1769–1821). Napoleon was a military genius and emperor of France, who conquered continental Europe in the 19th Century.

## Julius Caesar

Gaius Julius Caesar (100 BC–44 BC) was a Roman general and statesman who played a critical role in transforming the Roman Republic into the Roman Empire. Caesar began a civil war in 49 BC from which he emerged as the unrivaled leader of the Roman world.

## Charidemus

Charidemus (340 BC) was Greek mercenary leader of 4$^{th}$ century BC.

## Christopher Houston "Kit" Carson

Christopher Houston (1809–1868), often known as "Kit" Carson, was an American frontiersman. He also became widely known for his role as John C. Fremont's guide in the American West.

## Winston Churchill

Sir Winston Churchill (1874–1965) was a British soldier, politician and statesman known for his leadership of the United Kingdom during World War II.

## Gen. Mark Clark

Mark Wayne Clark (1896–1984) was the youngest lieutenant (three-star) general in the U.S. Army. He served both World War II and the Korean War.

## Karl von Clausewitz

Karl von Clausewitz (1780–1831) was a Prussian general, military strategian and theoretician who stressed the moral and political aspects of war.

## Georges Clemenceau

Georges Clemenceau (1841–1929) was the Prime Minister of France during World War I who was instrumental in drafting the Treaty of Versailles

## Crazy Horse

Crazy Horse (literally "His-Horse-Is-Crazy" or "His-Horse-Is-Spirited") (1840 –1877) was a Native American leader of the Oglala Lakota. He took up arms against the U.S. Federal government to fight against encroachments on the territories of the Lakota people. Crazy Horse was also responsible for leading a war party at the Battle of Little Bighorn in June 1876.

## Oliver Cromwell

Oliver Cromwell (1599–1658) was an English military and political leader who was known for helping transform England from a monarchy into a republic during the English civil war.

## Captain Henry P. "Jim" Crowe

Captain Henry P. Crow "Jim" (1899–1991) was one of the most famous Marines of World War II. In the course of his military service he received the Silver Star, Navy Cross and a Purple Heart.

## Cyrus the Great

Cyrus (576–530 BC) also known as "Cyrus the Great" was the founder of the Persian Empire under the Achaemenid dynasty. He is often reffered to as the "Father of the Iranian Nation."

## Gunnery Sergeant Dan Daly

Considered the best in the business, Gunnery Sergeant Dan Daly "Dan" (1873–1937) was a legendary United States marine who received the Medal of Honor twice.

## King Darius III

Darius III (380–330 BC) was the king of ancient Persia who fought Alexander the Great and was defeated.

## King David

King David (1040-970 BC) was the second king of Israel.

## Demaratus

Demaratus (ruled 515–491 BC) was a king of Sparta who, in spite of his origins, was known for his opposition to a co-ruling Spartan king.

## Dieneces

Dieneces (died 480 BC) was one of the 300 Spartans who fought in the battle of Thermopylae under King Leonidas. Little is known about him apart from his legendary courage. The historian Herodotus states that he was known for other wise and witty sayings but these, unfortunately, have been lost.

## Sir Francis Drake

Sir Francis Drake (1540–1596) was a famous British sea captain, explorer privateer, navigator, slave trader and a politician of the Elizabethan era. Drake is known for helping defeat the Spanish Armada and for being the first Englishman to sail around the world.

## Dwight D. Eisenhower

Dwight D. Eisenhower (1890–1969) was the commander of the US forces in Europe during World War II. He commanded the successful Allied invasion of North Africa, France and Italy. After the war, Eisenhower became supreme commander of the NATO forces in Europe, and later successfully ran for President of the United States.

## Admiral David Glasgow Farragut

Admiral David Glasgow Farragut (1801-1870), Admiral David Glasgow Farragut (1801-1870) was a flag officer of the US Navy during the American Civil War.

## Ferdinand Foch

Ferdinand Foch (1851–1929) was a French soldier, military theorist and writer.

## General Nathan Bedford Forrest

Nathan Bedford Forrest (1821–1877) was a lieutenant general in the Confederate Army during the American Civil War. He was considered by many to be one of the best cavalry commanders during the Civil War.

## Frederick the Great

Fredrick the Great (1712–1786) was the King of Prussia from the Hohenzollern dynasty.

## General Gage

Thomas Gage (1719–1787) was a British general and military commander in the early days of the American War of Independence.

## Genghis Khan

Genghis Khan (1162–1227) was a 13th century military leader who founded the Mongol Empire.

## Ulysses S. Grant

General Ulysses S. Grant (1822–1885) was a Civil War commander and 18th President of the United States.

## Lord Haig

Lord Haig (1861–1928) was the Commander-in-Chief of the British forces in France during World War I.

## Hannibal

Hannibal (248–183 BC) was a Carthaginian general and tactician credited for being the most talented commanders in history.

## Sir Basil Henry Liddell Hart

Sir Basil Henry Liddell Hart (1895-1970) was an English soldier, military historian and leading inter-war theorist.

## Patrick Henry

Patrick Henry (1736–1799) was a politician and orator responsible for leading the movement for independence in Virginia in the 1770s.

# Henry V

Henry V of England (1387–1422) was the ruler of England during the Hundred Years' War with France. He was known for his military prowess, most notably at the Battle of Agincourt.

# Horace

Quintus Horatius Flaccus (65–8 BC) also known in English as Horace, was a Roman lyric poet during the time of Augustus.

# Stonewall Jackson

Thomas Jonathan "Stonewall" Jackson (1824-1863) was one of the most well-known Confederate commanders during the American Civil War.

# Thomas Jefferson

Thomas Jefferson (1743–1826) was third President of the United States and one of the Founding Fathers who drafted the Declaration of Independence.

# Joan of Arc

Saint Joan of Arc or The Maid of Orléans (1412–1431) was considered a national heroine of France as well as a Catholic Saint who led the French army to several critical victories during the Hundred Years' War.

# John Paul Jones

Admiral John Paul Jones (1747–1792) was the first naval fighter recorded in the American Revolutionary War. He was often referred to as the "Father of the American Navy."

# Joshua

Joshua (1450–1370 BC) was the leader of the Israelite tribes after the death of Moses.

## Uesugi Kenshin

Uesugi Kenshin (1530–1578) was a powerful warlord during the Sengoku period in Japan.

## Labayu

Labayu was the king of Shechem in the Middle East in 14<sup>th</sup> century BCE. He was a ruler under the pharaohs and had the responsibility of guarding prisoners of the Egyptian crown.

## Captain James Lawrence

James Lawrence (1781–1813) was an American naval officer who was involved in the war of 1812 where he commanded the USS Chesapeake in a single-ship action against HMS Shannon.

## Lawrence of Arabia

T. E. Lawrence, known as Lawrence of Arabia (1888–1935) was a British Army officer who served as a British liaison officer during the Arab Revolt of 1916-1918.

## General Robert E. Lee

Robert Edward Lee (1807–1870) was an American soldier and General who is best known for commanding the Confederate Army of North Virginia during the American Civil War.

## Leonidas

Leonidas (540–480 BC) was the king of Sparta who led the Spartan troops at the battle of Thermopylae against the Persian forces under Xerxes.

## Abraham Lincoln

Abraham Lincoln (1809–1865) was the 16th President of the United States who led the country through the American Civil war. Among his many accomplishments, Lincoln was known for preserving the Union and ending slavery.

## Lt Col. Tiwi Love

Lt. Col. Tiwi Love, first Commander of D company of the Maori Battalion, fought in Greece, Italy and Northern Africa during World War II.

## Lieutenant General Victor H. Krulak

Victor H. Krulak (1913–2008) was a US Marine who saw action in World War II, the Korean War and the Vietnam War. He also authored the book *First to Fight: An Inside View of the U.S. Marine Corps*, published in 1991. He received a number of decorations during his military career, including the Bronze Star, Navy Cross and the Navy Distinguished Service Medal.

## Judas Maccabeus

Judas Maccabeus was active around 160 BC. He was also known as Judah Maccabee, also spelled Machabeus, or Maccabaeus and "Judah the Hammer." Maccabeus led the Maccabean revolt against the Seleucid Empire (167-160 BCE). He is considered by many to be one of the greatest warriors in Jewish history alongside the likes of David, Joshua and Gideon.

## Machiavelli

Niccolo Machiavelli (1469–1527) was an Italian diplomat, philosopher, humanist and writer during the Renaissance. He wrote two highly influential works, *The Prince*, which outlines principles of government; and *The Art of War,* which outlines military strategy and techniques.

## Douglas MacArthur

General Douglas MacArthur (1880–1964) was an American General of the Philippine Army who played a critical role in the Pacific theater during World War II.

## Mao Zedong

Mao Zedong (1893–1976) was the leader of the People's Liberation Army and the Communist Party in China as well as a guerrilla warfare strategist, political theorist and author.

## Anthony McAuliffe

General Anthony McAuliffe (1898–1975) was the commander of the US 101$^{st}$ Airborne Division during the Battle of the Bulge during World War II.

## General George C. Marshall

General George C. Marshall (1880–1959) is considered to be America's foremost soldier during World War II. He served as chief of staff from 1939 to 1945, and acted as Secretary of State from 1947 to 1949, formulating the Marshall Plan, which provided economic and military aid to foreign nations.

## Bernard Law Montgomery

Bernard Law Montgomery (1887–1976) was a British military leader who played a prominent role in the Allied victories in Africa and Europe during World War II.

## Lord Moran

Charles McMoran Wilson, 1st Baron Moran, known as Lord Moran (1882–1977) was Sir Winston Churchill's personal physician who saved Churchill's life in 1943.

## Yagyu Munenori

Yagyu Munenori (1571–1646) was a Japanese swordsman who founded the Edo branch of Yagyū Shinkage-ryū (one of the oldest Japanese schools of swordsmanship).

## Audie Murphy

Audie Leon Murphy (1924–1971) was the most decorated U.S. soldier for World War II. By the end of the war, Murphy had killed 240 German soldiers and was wounded three times. Murphy appeared in more than 40 films, wrote poetry, and continually battled with post-traumatic stress disorder. Sadly, Murphy died in a plane crash in 1971 and was interred with full military honors in Arlington National Cemetery.

## Sir Charles Napier

Sir Charles Napier (1782–1853) was a British general and statesman who conquered Sind (now in Pakistan) and served as its governor.

## Horatio Nelson

Horatio Nelson (1758–1805) was Britain's greatest sailor and the victor at the battle of Trafalgar.

## Wilfred Owen

Wilfred Owen (1893 –1918) fought in the trenches of World War I for the British Army. Along with Siegfried Sassoon, he is remembered for his graphic poems about life and death in the front lines and in the trenches.

## Captain John Parker

John Parker (1729–1775) was an American farmer and soldier who commanded the Lexington militia at the Battle of Lexington in 1775.

## General Patton

George Smith Patton, Jr. (1885–1945) was an outspoken United States Army General who commanded corps and armies during World War II.

## John Pershing

General John Joseph "Black Jack" Pershing (1860–1948) was a General in the US Army during World War I.

## Philippe de Navarre

Philippe de Navarre (1336–1363) was the brother and supporter of Charles II of Navarre. Philippe undertook negotiations with Edward III of England, and brokered a treaty that lasted a reasonable amount of time.  After his brother's conflict with King John II of France was resolved, Philippe continued to fight against the mercenary troops that threatened the countryside.

## Colin Powell

Colin Powell (1937–present) was a four-star General in the United States Army and also served as Secretary of State under George W. Bush.

## Col. William Prescott

William Prescott (1726–1795) was an American colonel in the Revolutionary War who commanded the rebel troops in the Battle of Bunker Hill.

## Publius Flavius Vegetius Renatus

Publius Flavius Vegetius Renatus (4th century AD) was the author of *De Re Militari,* a four-volume treatise of strategy and tactics used by the Roman legions.

## Lewis Burwell "Chesty" Puller

Lieutenant General Lewis Burwell "Chesty" Puller (1898–1971) was the most decorated U.S. Marine in history who received five Navy Crosses.

## Pyrrhus

Pyrrhus or Pyrrhos (318–272 BC) was a Greek general of the Hellenistic era who later became Ling of Epirus and Macedon.

## Wu Qi

Wu Qi (440–381BC) was a Chinese military leader and strategist during the Warring State period.

## Franklin D. Roosevelt

Franklin Delano Roosevelt (1882–1945) was the 32nd President of the United States who helped encourage and inspire the American troops to fight against the German and Japanese forces during World War II.

## Robert the Bruce

Robert the Bruce (1274–1329) is considered to be one of the greatest kings of Scotland who rose to power during a turbulent time in Scotland's history.

## Roger I of Sicily

Roger I of Sicily (1031–1101) also known as "The Great Count", was the last great leader of the Norman conquest of southern Italy.

## Erwin Rommel

Erwin Rommel (1891–1944) also known as the "Desert Fox", was a famous and highly respected German Field Marshal of World War II.

## Saladin

Saladin (1138–1193 AD) was the leader of the Muslim/Saracen forces during the conflicts of the Crusades.

## Siegfried Sassoon

Siegfried Sassoon (1886–1967) served in the trenches of World War I fighting in the British forces. He wrote about his wartime experiences and is considered to be one of the most significant "soldier poets" of World War I.

## Norman Schwarzkopf, Jr.

General Herbert Norman Schwarzkopf, Jr. (1934–present) also known as "Stormin" Norman served as Commander of the U.S. Central Command and was commander of the Coalition Forces in the Persian Gulf War of 1991.

## Shaka Zulu

Shaka kaSenzangakhona (1787 – 1828) also known as Shaka Zulu, was considered by many to be the most influential leader of the Zulu Kingdom and one of the greatest Zulu chieftains. He is also credited for uniting many of the Northern Nguni people, specifically the Mtetwa Paramountcy and the Ndwandwe into the Zulu Kingdom. Shaka

Zulu has also been called a military genius for his reforms and innovations and condemned for the extreme brutality of his reign.

## General William T Sherman

William Tecumseh Sherman (1820–1891) was an American General in the Union Army during the American Civil War.

## Huang Shi Gong

Huang Shi Gong (200 BC) was a military advisor and teacher to Zhang Liang, who was advisor to the emperor of the Han Dynasty. Huang Shi Gong authored the *Three Strategies*, which is considered to be one of the seven key Chinese military manuals.

## Shiba Yoshimasa

Shiba Yoshimasa (1350-1410) was a feudal lord during the Namboku and Muromachi Periods who wrote "The Chikubasho," a set of precepts for the young men of his clan.

## Admiral Earl St Vincent

John Jervis (1735–1823) was an admiral in the British Royal Navy and member of Parliament in the United Kingdom.

## Sun Bin

Sun Bin (died 316 BC) served as a military strategist in the Qi state during the Warring States Period. He wrote the military treatise known as *"Sun Bin's Art of War"* which is often conflated with Sun Tzu's *"The Art of War"*.

## Sun Tzu

Sun Wu (544 BC–496 BC) also known as the Sun Tzu, was a Chinese general, strategist and philosopher who authored *"The Art of War"* – an ancient Chinese book on military strategy.

## Sir Philip Sydney

Sir Philip Sidney (1554–1586) was famous English poet, courtier and soldier who fought in the Battle of Zutphen.

## Tacitus

Publius Cornelius Tacitus (56–117 AD) was a Roman historian who compiled, among other works, the history of Agricola's campaigns in Britain (Agricola was Tacitus's father-in-law). This work praises the honesty and integrity of Agricola in his position of command as governor of Britain and commander of the Roman legions in Britain.

## Jiang Taigong

Jiang Taigong (Shang dynasty, 16th -11th century BC, exact date unknown) was a sage employed by King Wen of the Zhou state as an advisor in military matters. He wrote a treatise on military strategy known as *The Six Secret Strategic Teachings. Strategic Teachings* use fishing as analogy.

## Themistocles

Themistocles (524–459 BC) was a general in the Athenian army who commanded the Greek navy against the Persian forces of Xerxes.

## Thirty-Six Stratagems

The *Thirty-Six Stratagems* is a collection of essay on military and political strategy that was originally written in China some time before the Southern Qi Dynasty (479–502 AD). The exact author of the *Thirty-Six Stratagems* is unknown, but the work has been attributed to Sun Tzu and Zhuge Liang. The *Thirty-Six Stratagems* do not actually contain 36 techniques for warfare; the number has been chosen as symbolizing completeness.

## Thucydides

Thucydides (c. 460 BC–395 BC) was a Greek historian who fought for the Greeks in the Peloponnesian War.

## Tokugawa Ieyasu

Tokugawa Ieyasu (1543–1616) was the first shogun of Tokugawa in Japan. He seized power by force and later formed a military alliance with Takeda Shingen. He wrote a compendium of instructions for his daimyo (lords), containing principles of life for warriors.

## Lt. Col. W. Barrett Travis

William Barret Travis (1809–1836) was the Texas commander at the Battle of the Alamo.

## Vercingetorix

Vercingetorix (82–46 BC) was the ruler of the Averni tribe of Gauls who stood against the invasions of Julius Caesar.

## William Wallace

William Wallace (1272 - 1305) was a Scottish knight and patriot who led his country against the English occupation of Scotland and who became one of the primary leaders during the Wars of Scottish Independence.

## George Washington

George Washington (1732–1799) was the commander in chief of the Continental Army during 1775–1783 and led America to victory over Britain in the American Revolutionary War. He was also unanimously elected the first President of the United States of America.

## Sir Arthur Wellesley, Duke of Wellington

Arthur Wellesley (1769–1852) was an Anglo-Irish statesman and soldier who is considered to be one of the leading military and political figures of the 19th century.

## Kaiser Wilhelm II

Kaiser Wilhelm II (1859–1941) was the 9th King of Prussia and the 3rd Emperor of Germany. Despite the fact he was Queen Victoria's grandson, Wilhelm pursued an anti-British foreign policy and supported South Africa during the Boer War. Wilhelm was Commander-in-Chief of the armed forces during the First World War.

## Xenophon

Xenophon (430–354 BC) was a mercenary soldier from Athens during the Classical Greek period, fighting for the Persian king Cyrus.

## Isoroku Yamamoto

Admiral Isoroku Yamamoto (1884–1943) was the commander-in-chief of the Combined Fleet of the Japanese Navy during World War II. He is chiefly remembered for instigating the plot to bomb Pearl Harbor and masterminding the strategies used during the Battle of Midway.

# About The Author

Sammy Franco is one of the world's foremost authorities on armed and unarmed combat. Highly regarded as a leading innovator in combat sciences, Mr. Franco was one of the premier pioneers in the field of "reality-based" self-defense. Convinced of the limited usefulness of martial arts in real street fighting situations, Mr. Franco believes in the theory that the best way to change traditional thinking is to make antiquated ideas obsolete through superior methodology. His innovative ideas have made a significant contribution to changing the thinking of many in the field about how people can best defend themselves against vicious and formidable adversaries.

Sammy Franco is perhaps best known as the founder and creator of Contemporary Fighting Arts (CFA), a state-of-the-art offensive-based combat system that is specifically designed for real-world self-defense. CFA is a sophisticated and practical system of self-defense, designed specifically to provide efficient and effective methods to avoid, defuse, confront, and neutralize both armed and unarmed attackers.

After studying and training in numerous martial art systems and related disciplines and acquiring extensive firsthand experience from real "street" combat, Mr. Franco developed his first system, known as *Analytical Street Fighting*. This system, which was one of the first practical "street fighting" martial arts, employed an unrestrained reality-based training methodology known as Simulated Street Fighting. Analytical Street Fighting served as the foundation for the fundamental principles of Contemporary Fighting Arts and Mr. Franco's teaching methodology. CFA also draws from the concepts and principles of numerous sciences and disciplines, including police and military science, criminal justice, criminology, sociology, human psychology, philosophy, histrionics, kinesics, proxemics, kinesiology, emergency medicine, crisis management, and human anatomy.

Sammy Franco has frequently been featured in martial art magazines, newspapers, and appeared on numerous radio and television programs. Mr. Franco has also authored numerous magazine articles and editorials, and has developed a popular library of instructional DVDs and workout music.

Mr. Franco has also written numerous best-selling books, including his first book, *Street Lethal*, released in 1989, which was one of the first books ever written on the subject of reality based self defense. His other books include *Killer Instinct, When Seconds Count, 1001 Street Fighting Secrets, First Strike, The Bigger They Are – The Harder They Fall, War Machine, War Craft, and Ground War.*

Sammy Franco's experience and credibility in the combat science is unequaled. One of his many accomplishments in this field includes the fact that he has earned the ranking of a Law Enforcement Master Instructor, and has designed, implemented, and taught officer survival training to the United States Border Patrol (USBP). He instructs members of the US Secret Service, Military Special Forces, Washington DC Police Department, Montgomery County, Maryland Deputy Sheriffs, and the US Library of Congress Police. He is a member of the prestigious American Society of Law Enforcement Trainers (ASLET) and he is listed in the "Who's Who Director of Law Enforcement Instructors."

Sammy Franco is a nationally certified Law Enforcement Instructor in the following curricula: PR-24 Side-Handle Baton, Police Arrest and Control Procedures, Police Personal Weapons Tactics, Police Power Handcuffing Methods, Police Oleoresin Capsicum Aerosol Training (OCAT), Police Weapon Retention and Disarming Methods, Police Edged Weapon Countermeasures and "Use of Force" Assessment and Response Methods. Mr. Franco is also a nationally certified firearm instructor (both police and civilian) who specializes in firearm safety, personal protection, and advanced combat shooting.

Mr. Franco holds a Bachelor of Arts degree in Criminal Justice from the University of Maryland. He is a regularly featured speaker at a number of professional conferences, and conducts dynamic and enlightening seminars on numerous aspects of self-defense and personal protection. Mr. Franco has instructed thousands of students in his career, including instruction on "street fighting", grappling and ground fighting, boxing and kickboxing, knife survival and knife fighting skills, multiple opponent survival skills, stick fighting skills and firearms training.

Sammy Franco teaches not only combat-proven techniques, but from the standpoint of having a firsthand understanding of the emotional, psychological and spiritual issues that arise from surviving physical violence. Having lived through violence himself, Mr. Franco's goal is not its glorification, but to help people free themselves from violence and its costly price. For more information about Mr. Franco, you can visit his website at: www.sammyfranco.com